ECOLOGY, LIBERTY & PROPERTY

ECOLOGY, LIBERTY & PROPERTY:

A Free Market Environmental Reader

Jonathan H. Adler, Editor

COMPETITIVE ENTERPRISE INSTITUTE

Washington, D.C.

ISBN 1-889865-02-8

Printed in the United States of America.

COMPETITIVE ENTERPRISE INSTITUTE
1001 Connecticut Avenue, N.W.
Suite 1250
Washington, D.C., 20036

Cover design by Barnett Danner
Layout by Dyann Collins

Contents

❖ ❖ ❖

Pollution Control

Risk Issues

Preface

❖ ❖ ❖

Environmental policy has been an integral part of the Competitive Enterprise Institute's research and advocacy portfolio since its founding in 1984. CEI President and founder Fred L. Smith, Jr., himself served as an analyst at the Environmental Protection Agency and was deeply concerned that defenders of free enterprise and limited government devoted inadequate time and attention to environmental concerns. In both intellectual and political contexts, too many were willing to accept the idea that only centralized government regulation is capable of safeguarding environmental concerns. Neither major party, and few political leaders, dared to broach an alternative vision. Ceding this moral high ground facilitated the unchecked expansion of federal environmental regulation throughout the 1970s and 1980s—something from which both economy and ecology suffered.

The environmental policy program has been the Institute's largest department through most of the Institute's history. It has also been the most influential. Over the past sixteen years, CEI's environmental policy program has played a central role in the development of free market approaches to environmental protection, producing numerous books, studies, reports, and articles documenting the failings of environmental regulation and the promise of free market alternatives.

This volume presents a small selection of essays on a range of environmental topics from CEI's first sixteen years of work on environmental policy issues. Organized by general subject matter, they range from the fairly theoretical to the highly practical. Together they represent a vision of environmental protection that relies upon the institutions of a free society—private property, contract, voluntary exchange, and the rule of law—rather than the coercive tools of a regulatory state. They represent a policy agenda that advances environmental protection without sacrificing individual liberty.

Many individuals have contributed to the development of CEI's environmental work over the past sixteen years. In addition to the authors of the selections in this volume, CEI's environmental policy efforts have benefited from the contributions of Ebere Akobundu, Ronald Bailey, David Barrett, James Bovard, David Crawford, Clyde Wayne Crews, Christopher Culp, Kimberle Dodd, Myron Ebell, Kelly Von Glenn, Michael Greve, Matthew Hoffman, Kent Jeffreys, Gordon Jones, Sam Kazman, Lee Kessler, Gregory Koontz, Kathy Kushner, Marlo Lewis, Ben Lieberman, Angela Logomasini, Daniel McInnis, Mark Mills, Richard Miniter, George Pieler, David Riggs, Michael Sanera, Brian Seasholes, Daniel Simmons, Jonathan Tolman, Michael Vivoli, Anthony Woodlief, and Jennifer Zambone, among others. Their contributions have been as important to the development of CEI's environmental policy agenda as those whose names appear on the articles herein.

In addition to the aforementioned individuals and authors, this book would not have been possible without the expert layout and editorial assistance of Dyann Collins. Additional editorial review was provided by Max Schulz and Kendra Okonski. And, as with all CEI's environmental efforts, none of this would be possible without the inspiration and guidance of Fred L. Smith, Jr.

— Jonathan H. Adler
March 2000

Introduction

❖ ❖ ❖

Jonathan H. Adler

Federal air quality regulations mandate the use of fuel additives that increase the cost of gasoline yet produce no significant improvements in air quality. These additives are not without their environmental impacts, however, as one reduces one set of emissions at the expense of increasing another, and a second has caused widespread groundwater contamination.

Regulatory protection for endangered species discourages habitat conservation on private land. Stringent land-use restrictions make ownership of endangered-species habitat a liability instead of an asset, and landowners respond accordingly. In over 25 years, more species have become extinct under these regulatory "protections" than have been recovered.

A federal program for the cleanup of hazardous waste sites spends more on lawyers and paperwork than on reducing risks to public health. Since the creation of "Superfund," cleanup costs have skyrocketed to over $25 million per site. Worse for neighboring communities, the average cleanup takes over a decade.

Under the Clean Water Act, a private company can be fined $25,000 per day for a technical paperwork

Portions of this essay are adapted from Jonathan H. Adler, *Environmentalism at the Crossroads* © 1995 Capital Research Center.

*violation that produces no environmental impact
whatsoever. At the same time, the law bars well-
founded common law actions over interstate water
pollution.*

*Federal mandates for automobile fuel efficiency force
automakers to produce cars and light trucks that are
smaller and lighter—and therefore less safe—than
they would otherwise be. According to a Harvard-
Brookings study, these regulations cause an
additional 2,000 to 4,000 highway fatalities each
year.*

There is something terribly wrong with the current regime
of environmental regulations. Environmental statutes and
regulations designed to protect environmental quality are failing.
Even laws that produced environmental gains in the 1970s are no
longer up to the task. The result is a costly regulatory regime that
undermines the goal of environmental protection.

The fundamental problem with existing environmental laws
is that they embody a command-and-control, government-knows-
best mentality. Conventional policy approaches proceed from the
assumption that markets "fail" to address environmental concerns.
Government intervention is called for wherever market activities
impact environmental quality. Yet there is no end to the range of
private activities which generate environmental effects, and
centralized regulatory agencies are ill-equipped to handle myriad
ecological interactions triggered or impacted by private activity. As
environmental analyst Richard Stewart noted, "the system has grown
to the point where it amounts to nothing less than a massive effort at
Soviet-style planning of the economy to achieve environmental
goals."[1]

Stewart's description is particularly apt. The Soviet
economic model, like the conventional approach to environmental

protection, was able to produce gains for a time. Collectivized agriculture did produce wheat—at least in the beginning. Over time, however, centrally-planned systems collapsed under their own weight, revealing a bankrupt core. As with the economic planning of the former Soviet nations, so too with the ecological planning of the federal regulatory state. There is a growing consensus that federal regulatory policies are too costly and ineffective. Regulations passed in the 1960s and 1970s are no longer generating satisfactory results. In many cases, well-intentioned regulatory systems are even making environmental problems worse.

Dissatisfied with the *status quo* approach to environmental policy, a growing number of scholars and policy analysts are turning to the marketplace to address environmental concerns. They have found in what many call "free market environmentalism" a new set of policy approaches that reconcile human needs and environmental concerns. Grounded in property rights, voluntary exchange, common law liability protections, and the rule of law, free market environmentalism seeks to integrate environmental resources into the market system. Rather than regulate each new potential risk to environmental quality, free market environmentalists advocate the creation of institutional arrangements that facilitate private solutions to environmental concerns. Markets are not perfect, but they are superior to the regulatory alternative.

New Resource Economics

Why do government agencies have such a poor record managing natural resources and public lands? This was the question posed by the economists who initially developed the ideas of free market environmentalism. "If qualified managers with good intentions were sufficient to ensure sound decisionmaking, Yellowstone would be the Eden of the national parks," observed Michael Copeland, former executive director of the Bozeman, Montana-based Political Economy Research Center (PERC).[2] But it was widely recognized that Yellowstone National Park was grossly mismanaged. As environmental writer Alston Chase poignantly documented in *Playing God in Yellowstone*, "rather than preserved, [the park] is being destroyed," and public management is to blame.[3] "The experiment of public sector ownership, management and control has been an unambiguous failure in terms of environmental quality, productivity and economic efficiency," decided John Baden, PERC's first executive director who later established the Foundation for Research on Economics and the Environment (FREE).[4]

Baden cautioned critics of the federal bureaucracy that agency employees were neither incompetent nor immoral. The problem is, rather, that government officials and staff respond only too well to the signals government sends. "All decisions in an agency are made on the basis of information and incentives," Baden concluded. "Current institutions systematically generate both bad information and perverse incentives."[5]

PERC executive director Terry Anderson argued that conventional natural resource economics is analytically biased in favor of government regulation. It assumes that "market failure is pervasive in natural resource allocation and that cost/benefit analysis applied by scientific, objective managers can improve on the failures."[6] To challenge the conventional wisdom, analysts at PERC and elsewhere developed a "New Resource Economics" (NRE) which explains how institutional arrangements such as private ownership affect incentives and environmental outcomes. NRE applies the insights of Nobel economics laureates F.A. Hayek, Ronald Coase, and James Buchanan to natural resource questions. Copeland explained: "NRE developed from a concern for the environment, the integrity of which was being compromised—not only by seemingly irresponsible individuals, but by the very government agencies assigned to protect the environment!"[7]

NRE demonstrated that public officials act in their self-interest no less than individuals in the private sector, and that bad government policies result because, unlike private decisionmaking in the marketplace, public officials are not rewarded for efficiency or punished for waste. "Wasting a resource does not result in a loss or a reduced profit," said Copeland of government bureaucracy. "Bureaucrats also tend to favor programs with visible benefits and invisible costs."[8]

Lacking the price signals of profit and loss, public officials rarely have the information they need to plan complex systems and allocate resources. Hence, they cannot anticipate how various institutional arrangements will affect the incentives that motivate individuals. But this is necessary if we want to understand the likely impact of specific environmental programs and policies. NRE demonstrated that government failure was likely to be as pervasive as, if not more than, market imperfections. An intellectual discipline, the New Resource Economics set the theoretical groundwork for free market environmentalism.

The Theory of Free Market Environmentalism

Conventional environmental policymaking presupposes that only government action can improve environmental quality. In this view, environmental problems arise from "market failures" that produce "externalities." Government regulation is needed to correct environmental concerns that the market has "failed" to handle because they are "external" to the price signals that regulate marketplace transactions. The conventional paradigm of environmental policy justifies the regulation of economic activity because it assumes all activities—from purchasing clothing to driving a car to turning on a light bulb—have an impact on the environment that is not factored into the cost of the product or service. Economic central planning may be intellectually and historically discredited, but the "market failure" thesis justifies environmental central planning, an endeavor just as prone to ruin. In the words of Competitive Enterprise Institute president Fred L. Smith, Jr., "The disastrous road to serfdom can just as easily be paved with green bricks as with red ones."[9] Embracing the "market failure" rationale leads to policy failure.

Free market environmentalism (FME) rejects the "market failure" model. "Rather than viewing the world in terms of market failure, we should view the problem of externalities as a *failure to permit markets* and create markets where they do not yet—or no longer—exist," argues Smith.[10] Resources that are privately owned or managed and, therefore, are in the marketplace are typically well-maintained. Resources that are unowned or politically controlled, and therefore outside the market, are more apt to be inadequately managed. "At the heart of free market environmentalism is a system of well-specified property rights to natural resources," explain Terry Anderson and Donald Leal, authors of *Free Market Environmentalism.*[11] Adds Smith, "Rather than the silly slogan of some environmentalists, that 'trees should have standing,' our argument is that behind every tree should stand an owner who can act as its protector."[12]

FME owes an intellectual debt to ecologist Garrett Hardin's discussion of the "tragedy of the commons."[13] Hardin noted when a resource is unowned or owned in common, such as the grazing pasture in a medieval village, there is no incentive for any individual to protect it. In the medieval village it is in every cattleowner's self-interest to have his herd graze the pasture as much as possible and before any other herd. Every cattleowner who acquires additional cattle gains the benefits of a larger herd, while the cost of overusing the pasture is borne by all members of the village. Inevitably, the consequence is an overgrazed pasture, and everyone loses. Indeed, the cattleowner with foresight will anticipate that the pasture will become barren in the future, and this will give him additional incentive to overgraze. Refusing to add another cow to one's own herd does not change the incentive of every other cattleowner to do so.

The world's fisheries offer a contemporary example of the tragedy of the commons. Because oceans are unowned, each fishing fleet has no incentive to conserve or replenish the fish it takes and it has every incentive to take as many fish as possible lest the benefits of a larger catch go to someone else.[14] Private ownership overcomes the commons problem because owners can prevent overuse by controlling access to the resource. As Hardin noted, "The tragedy of the commons as a food basket is averted by private property, or something formally like it."[15]

Although environmental activists often disparage private ownership, the record of private owners in conserving resources is superior to that of government agencies. For instance, Terry Anderson observes that "well-established private rights to Great Lakes timber resulted in efficient markets rather than the 'rape and run' tactics alleged by conservationists."[16] As R.J. Smith explains,

> Wherever we have exclusive private ownership, whether it is organized around a profit-seeking or nonprofit undertaking, there are incentives for the private owners to preserve the resource....[P]rivate ownership allows the owner to capture the full capital value of the resource, and self-interest and economic incentive drive the owner to maintain its long-term capital value.[17]

Unlike public officials, private owners directly benefit from sound management decisions and suffer from poor ones.

For incentives to work, the property right to a resource must be definable, defendable, and divestible. Owners must be free to transfer their property rights to others at will. Even someone indifferent or hostile to environmental protection has an incentive to take environmental concerns into account, because despoiling the resource may reduce its value in the eyes of potential buyers. The role of government is to protect property rights for environmental resources and secure the voluntary agreements property owners contract to carry out. Moreover, FME advocates insist on the application of common law liability rules to environmental harms, such as polluting a neighbor's property, to protect property rights and to provide additional incentives for good stewardship. To harm someone's property by polluting it is no more acceptable than vandalizing it.

The importance of private ownership to sound conservation is clear from America's environmental history. When environmental groups like the National Audubon Society and the Nature Conservancy act to protect habitat and ecologically sensitive areas by purchasing land and establishing sanctuaries, they act in the marketplace to advance environmental values. R.J. Smith explains:

> Private ownership includes not only hunting preserves, commercial bird breeders, parrot jungles, and safari parks, it also includes wildlife sanctuaries, Audubon Society refuges, World Wildlife Fund preserves, and a multitude of private, non-profit conservation and preservation projects.[18]

These organizations raise money by soliciting contributions to acquire ownership in preferred lands. Were it not for the institution of private property, these ventures to protect the environment would be impossible.

Private efforts to support the reintroduction of wolves in Montana offers another example of how market transactions can advance environmental goals. The hostility of ranchers has been a major obstacle to reintroducing predators into the wild. In the 1970s, free market economists argued that ranchers' fear of livestock losses would be addressed if those who wanted to reintroduce wolves would agree to compensate ranchers who suffered economic loss due to predators.[19]

Defenders of Wildlife adopted the idea and established a Wolf Compensation Fund. "What we're trying to do is devise a system whereby all those people who care about endangered species restoration actually pay some of the bills," explained Defenders of Wildlife staffer Hank Fischer. "What this solution attempts to do is utilize economic forces—in other words, to make it desirable to have wolves."[20] After several years, the fund had paid ranchers approximately $12,000 for livestock losses. The program has flaws—some ranchers complain that compensation is not always paid, and federal regulations still prevent ranchers from killing wolves to protect livestock—but the Fund remains an example of how marketplace transactions can further environmental goals even when no goods are exchanged.

FME proponents would terminate government programs that cause environmental harm or inhibit private-sector solutions to environmental problems. Free market environmental policies would establish property rights, where possible, so as to internalize "externalities." In some cases, FME proponents would counsel more modest steps. For instance, in the difficult case of automobile air pollution, a "polluter pays" approach would replace regulations mandating specific emissions-control equipment and annual emissions testing. An owner would be assessed a fee proportional to the amount of pollution his auto generated. Since fees would vary in relation to pollution emission levels, owners would have incentives to have their automobiles repaired or replaced when they began to pollute significantly. Technologies currently exist to monitor emissions as autos move on the highway, providing potential enforcement mechanisms that will not inconvenience most owners of vehicles whose emission levels are negligible. This solution is not ideal because a genuine market is not created; but it is more market-oriented that current air pollution policies.[21]

The Environmental Establishment's Response
Most environmental activists reject free market environmentalism. Economist Thomas Michael Power and *Sierra* associate editor Paul Rauber write: "Markets are not neutral, technological devices. They are social institutions whose use has profound consequences. All societies purposely limit the extent of the market in order to protect basic values."[22] Wedded to the state as

the instrument of reform, environmental activists cannot accept the idea that market forces will produce the results they desire even when it is apparent that government regulation will not.

Nonetheless, FME has changed the discussion of environmental issues. Many environmentalists now seem to understand why environmental policies should be examined in economic terms. Says Roberto Repetto, director of the economics program at World Resources Institute, "If we can enact policies that adjust prices so they more accurately reflect all the costs associated with producing a particular pollutant or using particular resources, then society will make better decisions."[23] Repetto advocates pollution taxes and other government interventions as ways to "internalize" externalities. Such policies are not FME, but they are evidence that the terms of debate are shifting.

Some environmentalists also see the strategic political benefit of market rhetoric and some free market policies. Ned Ford, energy chair of the Sierra Club's Ohio chapter, argues that "by forcing the marketplace to the lowest cost solution that really works, environmentalists gain credibility and enhance the opportunity for further reduction."[24] Even President Bill Clinton has acknowledged the importance of developing a "market-based environmental-protection strategy," noting that "Adam Smith's invisible hand can have a green thumb."[25] Too often, however, market rhetoric merely merchandises government regulatory policies. Environmentalist groups rarely adopt FME policies fully, opting instead to pick and choose free market precepts.

Attempts to use "market mechanisms" to reach predetermined environmental outcomes are the most common example of this tactic. The Environmental Defense Fund (EDF), for instance, advocates widespread use of "pollution credit trading" as a market-oriented policy. Setting an emission level as an environmental target, the EDF proposal allows companies the freedom to determine how best to reach it. Companies could buy and sell emission allotments among themselves to find the least-cost means to reach a goal set by government regulation. Explains EDF's Dan Dudek, "Who is better to know [what to do] than the people who own and operate" the facility causing pollution?[26]

FME advocates note that this approach will not necessarily produce sound environmental policy. The Clean Air Act Amendments of 1990, for instance, include an elaborate EDF-designed pollution-credit trading scheme for sulfur oxide emissions to control acid rain. Many companies favored the policy because, by allowing them to select the least-cost pollution reduction measures, they might save millions of dollars in compliance costs. But was a sulfur oxide emission reduction plan needed at all? The most extensive US study of acid rain to date suggests that acid rain was not a substantial threat to forests and streams, despite environmentalist claims to the contrary.

John Baden warns against market mechanisms that are used "simply as tools for the efficient delivery of environmental goals...[while] the goals themselves remain collectively determined."[27] CEI's Fred Smith calls such policies "market socialism," as they resemble the efforts in Communist countries to use market mechanisms to reach politically determined production quotas. EDF's emission trading scheme is structurally the equivalent of the tradeable wheat production quotas established in parts of Eastern Europe. Notes Smith, "the efficiency gains of market systems occur not only in production, but in allocation as well. This means that markets are as effective at determining what is to be done as they are at determining how it should be accomplished."[28]

The Road Ahead

Free market environmental policies will not soon be embraced by many environmental regulators, activists, or lobbyists. But the fact that "market" language—incentives, costs, trade-offs, markets, property rights, and so on—dominates current environmental discussions suggests that it presents a serious challenge to conventional environmental policy approaches. Even the most statist environmental activist organizations feel the need to embrace "market" perspectives on certain issues. As the editor of the Worldwatch Institute's book series seemed to lament in the introduction to a book on "market" mechanisms, "market economies will remain the dominant economic system for the foreseeable future."[29] Markets may well become the basis for the next generation of environmental protections as well.

Advancing the free market environmental agenda will certainly be a challenge. On top of the obvious political obstacles, there are serious implementation questions that need to be addressed. There are tremendous legal and cultural barriers to the extension of market institutions in many areas. The technical requirements of property rights definition and enforcement are also substantial. It is one thing to create rights in instream water flows, as is done in many states; it is quite another to contemplate property rights in the air or the deep seas. The relevant question, however, is whether these obstacles are any greater than asking the federal government to plan our collective environmental future. The experience with environmental policy to date suggests not. Central planning has clearly failed. It is time to give market institutions a chance.

Notes

1. Richard B. Stewart, "Controlling Environmental Risks Through Economic Incentives," *Columbia Journal of Environmental Law*, vol. 13, no. 153 (1988), p. 154.

2. Michael Copeland, "The New Resource Economics," in *The Yellowstone Primer*, J. Baden and D. Leal, eds. (San Francisco: Pacific Research Institute, 1990), p. 13.

3. Alston Chase, *Playing God in Yellowstone* (New York: Harcourt Brace, 1987), p. 6.

4. "Economists: Free Market Better for Resource Management," United Press International, November 19, 1983.

5. Ibid.

6. Terry L. Anderson, "The New Resource Economics: Old Ideas and New Applications," *American Journal of Agricultural Economics* (December 1982), p. 929.

7. Copeland, p. 14.

8. Ibid, pp. 17-18.

9. Fred L. Smith, Jr., "The Market and Nature," *The Freeman* (September 1993), p. 352 [see pp. 25-38 in this volume].

10. Fred L. Smith, Jr., "Conclusion: Environmental Policy at the Crossroads," in *Environmental Politics: Public Costs, Private Rewards* (New York: Praeger, 1992), p. 192 [see pp. 199-225 in this volume].

11. Terry L. Anderson and Donald R. Leal, *Free Market Environmentalism* (San Francisco: Pacific Research Institute, 1991), p. 3.

12. Fred Smith, "Conclusion," p. 192.

13. See Garrett Hardin, "The Tragedy of the Commons," *Science*, December 13, 1968.

14. See Kent Jeffreys, "Rescuing the Oceans," in *The True State of the Planet*, Ron Bailey, ed. (New York: The Free Press, 1995).

15. Hardin, p. 1243.

16. Anderson, "The New Resource Economics," p. 933.

17. R.J. Smith, "Resolving the Tragedy of the Commons by Creating Private Property Rights in Wildlife," *Cato Journal* (Fall 1981), pp. 456-457 [see pp. 101-110 in this volume].

18. Ibid., p. 456.

19. Ryan Amacher, et al., "The Economics of Fatal Mistakes: Fiscal Mechanisms for Preserving Endangered Predators," in *Wildlife in the Marketplace*, Terry Anderson and P.J. Hill, eds. (Lanham, Maryland: Rowman and Littlefield, 1995).

20. Quoted on "Free Market Environmentalism's Bottom Line," National Public Radio Morning Edition, September 1, 1992.

21. See Jonathan Adler, *Reforming Arizona's Air Pollution Policy* (Phoenix: Goldwater Institute, 1993).

22. Thomas Michael Power and Paul Rauber, "The Price is Everything," *Sierra* (November/December 1993), p. 94.

23. Joe Alper, "Protecting the Environment With the Power of the Market," *Science*, June 25, 1993, p. 1884.

24. Power and Rauber, p. 89.

25. Ibid., p. 88.

26. Karen Riley, "Rewards for Friends of the Earth," *Washington Times*, November 22, 1992.

27. Power and Rauber, p. 92.

28. Fred L. Smith, Jr., "Europe, Energy & the Environment: The Case Against Carbon Taxes" (Washington, DC: Competitive Enterprise Institute, 1992), p. 8 [see pp. 183-188 in this volume].

29. Linda Starke, "Foreword," in David Malin Roodman, *The Natural Wealth of Nations* (New York: W.W. Norton, 1998), p. 12.

❖ **A Primer on Free Market
Environmentalism**

The Market and Nature

Fred L. Smith, Jr.

Many environmentalists are dissatisfied with the environmental record of free economies. Capitalism, it is claimed, is a wasteful system, guilty of exploiting the finite resources of the Earth in a vain attempt to maintain a non-sustainable standard of living. Such charges, now raised under the banner of "sustainable development," are not new. Since Malthus made his dire predictions about the prospects for world hunger, the West has been continually warned that it is using resources too rapidly and will soon run out of something, if not everything. Nineteenth century experts such as W.S. Jevons believed that world coal supplies would soon be exhausted and would have been amazed that over 200 years of reserves now exist. US timber "experts" were convinced that North American forests would soon be a memory. They would similarly be shocked by the reforestation of eastern North America—reforestation that has resulted from market forces and not mandated government austerity.

In recent decades, the computer-generated predictions of the Club of Rome enjoyed a brief popularity, arguing that everything would soon disappear. Fortunately, most now recognize that such computer simulations, and their static view of resource supply and demand, have no relation to reality. Nevertheless, these models are back, most notably in the book *Beyond the Limits*, and enjoying their newly-found attention. This theme of imminent resource exhaustion has become a chronic element in the annual Worldwatch Institute publication, *State of the World*. (This book is, to my knowl-

Originally appeared in *The Freeman*, September 1993.

edge, the only gloom-and-doom book in history which advertises next year's edition.) Today, sustainable-development theorists from the World Bank's Herman Daly and the United Nations' Maurice Strong to Vice President Albert Gore and Canadian author David Suzuki, seem certain that, at last, Malthus will be proven right. It was this environmental view on display at the United Nations' "Earth Summit" in Rio de Janeiro in June, 1992. This conference, vast in scope and mandate, was but the first step in the campaign to make the environment the central organizing principle of global institutions.

If such views are taken seriously, then the future will indeed be a very gloomy place, for if such disasters are in the immediate future, than drastic government action is necessary. Consider the not atypical view of David Suzuki:

> [T]here has to be a radical restructuring of the priorities of society. That means we must no longer be dominated by global economics, that the notion that we must continue to grow indefinitely is simply off, that we must work towards, not zero growth, but negative growth.

For the first time in world history, the leaders of the developed nations are being asked to turn their backs on the future. The resulting policies could be disastrous for all mankind.

The Environmental Challenge

The world does indeed face a challenge in protecting ecological values. Despite tremendous success in many areas, many environmental concerns remain. The plight of the African elephant, the air over Los Angeles, the hillsides of Nepal, the three million infant deaths from water-borne diseases throughout the world, and the ravaging of Brazilian rain forests all dramatize areas where problems persist and innovative solutions are necessary.

Sustainable development theorists claim these problems result from "market failure": the inability of capitalism to address environmental concerns adequately. Free market proponents suggest such problems are not the result of market forces, but rather of their absence. The market already plays a critical role in protecting those resources which are privately owned and for which political interference is minimal. In these instances there are truly sustainable practices. Therefore, those concerned with protecting the environment and ensuring human prosperity should seek to expand capitalism, through the extension of property rights, to the broadest possible range of environmental resources. Our objective should be to reduce, not expand, political interference in both the human and natural environments.

Private stewardship of environmental resources is a powerful means of ensuring sustainability. Only people can protect the environment. Politics *per se* does nothing. If political arrangements fail to encourage individuals to play a positive role, the arrangements can actually do more harm than good. There are tens of millions of species of plants and animals that merit survival. Can we imagine that the 150 or so governments on this planet—many of which do poorly with their human charges—will succeed in so massive a stewardship task? Yet, there are in the world today over five billion people. Freed to engage in private stewardship, the challenge before them becomes surmountable.

Sustainable Development and Its Implications

The phrase *sustainable development* suggests a system of natural resource management that is capable of providing an equivalent, or expanding, output over time. As a concept, it is extremely vague, often little more than a platitude. Who, after all, favors non-sustainable development? The basic definition promoted by Gro

Harlem Brundtland, former Prime Minister of Norway and a prominent player at the 1992 Earth Summit, is fairly vague as well: "[S]ustainable development is a notion of discipline. It means humanity must ensure that meeting present needs does not compromise the ability of future generations to meet their own needs."

In this sense, sustainability requires that as resources are consumed one of three things must occur: New resources must be discovered or developed; demands must be shifted to more plentiful resources; or, new knowledge must permit us to meet such needs from the smaller resource base. That is, as resources are depleted, they must be renewed. Many assume that the market is incapable of achieving this result. A tremendous historical record suggests exactly the opposite.

Indeed, to many environmental "experts," today's environmental problems reflect the failure of the market to consider ecological values. This market-failure explanation is accepted by a panoply of political pundits of all ideological stripes, from Margaret Thatcher to Earth First! The case seems clear. Markets, after all, are short-sighted and concerned only with quick profits. Markets undervalue biodiversity and other ecological concerns not readily captured in the marketplace. Markets ignore effects generated outside of the market, so-called externalities, such as pollution. Since markets fail in these critical environmental areas, it is argued, political intervention is necessary. That intervention should be careful, thoughtful, even scientific, but the logic is clear: Those areas of the economy having environmental impacts must be politically controlled. Since, however, every economic decision has some environmental effect, the result is an effort to regulate the whole of human activity.

Thus, without any conscious decision being made, the world is moving decisively toward central planning for ecological rather than economic purposes. The Montreal Protocol on chlorofluoro-carbons, the international convention on climate change, the convention on biodiversity, and the full range of concerns addressed at the UN Earth Summit—all are indicative of this rush to politicize the world's economies. That is unfortunate, for ecological central planning is unlikely to provide for a greener world.

Rethinking the Market Failure Paradigm

The primary problem with the market-failure explanation is it demands too much. In a world of pervasive externalities—that is, a world where all economic decisions have environmental effects—this analysis demands all economic decisions be politically managed. The world is only now beginning to recognize the massive mistake entailed in economic central planning; yet, the "market failure" paradigm argues that we embark on an even more ambitious effort of ecological central planning. The disastrous road to serfdom can just as easily be paved with green bricks as with red ones.

That markets "fail" does not mean that governments will "succeed." Governments, after all, are susceptible to special interest pleadings. A complex political process often provides fertile ground for economic and ideological groups to advance their agendas at the public expense. The US tolerance of high-sulfur coal and the massive subsidies for heavily polluting "alternative fuels" are evidence of this problem. Moreover, governments lack any means of acquiring the detailed information dispersed throughout the economy essential to efficiency and technological change.

More significantly, if market forces were the dominant cause of environmental problems then the highly industrialized, capitalist countries should suffer from greater environmental problems than their centrally-managed counterparts. This was once the conventional wisdom. The Soviet Union, it was argued, would have no pollution because the absence of private property, the profit motive, and individual self-interest would eliminate the motives for harming the environment. The opening of the Iron Curtain exploded this myth, as the most terrifying ecological horrors ever conceived were shown to be the Communist reality. The lack of property rights and profit motivations discouraged efficiency, placing a greater stress on natural resources. The result was an environmental disaster.

Do Markets Fail—Or Do We Fail to Allow Markets?

John Kenneth Galbraith, an avowed proponent of statist economic policies, inadvertently suggested a new approach to environmental protection. In an oft-quoted speech he noted that the United States was a nation in which the yards and homes were beautiful and in which the streets and parks were filthy. Galbraith then went on to suggest that we effectively nationalize the yards and homes. For those of us who believe in property rights and economic liberty, the obvious lesson is quite the opposite.

Free market environmentalists seek ways of placing these properties in the care of individuals or groups concerned about their well-being. This approach does not, of course, mean that trees must have legal standing, but rather is a call for ensuring that behind every tree, stream, lake, air shed, and whale stands at least one owner who is able and willing to protect and nurture that resource.

Consider the plight of the African elephant. On most of the continent, the elephant is managed like the American buffalo once was. It remains a political resource. Elephants are widely viewed as the common heritage of all the peoples of these nations and are thus protected politically. The "common property" management strategy being used in Kenya and elsewhere in East and Central Africa has been compared and contrasted with the experiences of those nations such as Zimbabwe which have moved decisively in recent years to transfer elephant-ownership rights to regional tribal councils. The differences are dramatic. In Kenya, and indeed all of eastern Africa, elephant populations have fallen by over 50 percent in the last decade. In contrast, Zimbabwe's elephant population has been increasing rapidly. A program of conservation through use that relies upon uniting the interest of man and the environment succeeds where political management has failed.

The Market and Sustainability

The prophets of sustainability have consistently predicted an end to the world's abundant resources, while the defenders of the free market point to the power of innovation—innovation which is encouraged in the marketplace. Consider the agricultural experience. Since 1950, improved plant and animal breeds, expanded availability and types of agri-chemicals, innovative agricultural techniques, expanded irrigation, and better pharmaceutical products have all combined to spur a massive expansion of world food supplies. That was not expected by those now championing "sustainable development." Lester Brown, in his 1974 Malthusian publication *By Bread Alone*, suggested that crop-yield increases would soon cease. Since that date, Asian rice yields have risen nearly 40 percent, an approximate increase of 2.4 percent per year. This rate is similar to that of wheat and other grains. In the developed world it is food surpluses, not food shortages, that present the greater problem, while political institutions continue to obstruct the distribution of food in much of the Third World.

Man's greater understanding and ability to work with nature have made it possible to achieve a vast improvement in world food supplies, to improve greatly the nutritional levels of a majority of people throughout the world in spite of rapid population growth. Moreover, this has been achieved while reducing the stress to the environment. To feed the current world population at current nutritional levels using 1950 yields would require plowing under an additional 10 to 11 million square miles, almost tripling the world's agricultural land demands (now at 5.8 million square miles). This would surely come at the expense of land being used for wildlife habitat and other applications.

Moreover, this improvement in agriculture has been matched by improvements in food distribution and storage, again encouraged by natural market processes and the "profit incentive" that so many environmentalists deplore. Packaging has made it possible to reduce food spoilage, reduce transit damage, extend shelf life, and expand distribution regions. Plastic and other post-use wraps along with the ubiquitous Tupperware have further reduced food waste. As would be expected, the United States uses more packaging than Mexico, but the additional packaging results in tremendous reductions in waste. On average, a Mexican family discards 40 percent more waste each day. Packaging often eliminates more waste than it creates.

Despite the fact that capitalism has produced more environment-friendly innovations than any other economic system, the advocates of sustainable development insist that this process must be guided by benevolent government officials. That such efforts, such as the United States' synthetic fuels project of the late 1970s, have resulted in miserable failures is rarely considered. It is remarkable how many of the participants at the UN Earth Summit seemed completely oblivious to this historical reality.

In the free market, entrepreneurs compete in developing low-cost, efficient means to solve contemporary problems. The promise of a potential profit, and the freedom to seek after it, always provides the incentive to build a better mousetrap, if you will. Under planned economies, this incentive for innovation can never be as strong, and the capacity to reallocate resources toward more efficient means of production is always constrained.

This confusion is also reflected in the latest environmental fad: waste reduction. With typical ideological fervor, a call for increased efficiency in resource use becomes a call to use less of everything, regardless of the cost. Less, we are told, is more in terms of environmental benefit. But neither recycling nor material or energy use reductions *per se* are a good thing, even when judged solely on environmental grounds. Recycling paper often results in increased water pollution, increased energy use, and, in the United States, actually discourages the planting of new trees. Mandating increased fuel efficiency for automobiles reduces their size and weight, which in turn reduces their crashworthiness and increases highway fatalities. Environmental policies must be judged on their results, not just their motivations.

Overcoming Scarcity

Environmentalists tend to focus on ends rather than processes. This is surprising given their adherence to ecological teaching. Their obsession with the technologies and material-usage patterns of today reflects a failure to understand how the world works. The resources people need are not chemicals, wood fiber, copper, or the other raw materials of concern to the sustainable-development school. We demand housing, transportation, and communication services. How those demands are met is a derivative result based on competitive forces—forces which respond by suggesting new ways to meet old needs as well as improving the ability to meet needs in older ways.

Consider, for example, the fears expressed in the early post-war era that copper would soon be in short supply. Copper was the life-blood of the world's communication system, essential to linking together humanity throughout the world. Extrapolations suggested problems and copper prices escalated accordingly. The result? New sources of copper in Africa, South America, and even the United States and Canada, were found. That concern, however, also prompted others to review new technologies, an effort that produced today's rapidly expanding fiber optics links.

Such changes would be viewed as miraculous if not now commonplace in the industrialized, and predominantly capitalistic, nations of the world. Data assembled by Lynn Scarlett of the Reason Foundation noted that a system requiring, say, 1,000 tons of copper can be replaced by as little as 25 kilograms of silicon, the basic component of sand. Moreover, the fiber-optics system has the ability to carry over 1,000 times the information of the older copper wire. Such rapid increases in communication technology are also providing for the displacement of oil as electronic communication reduces the need to travel and commute. The rising fad of telecommuting was not dreamed up by some utopian environmental planner, but was rather a natural outgrowth of market processes.

It is essential to understand that physical resources are, in and of themselves, largely irrelevant. It is the interaction of man and science that creates resources: Sand and knowledge become fiber optics. Humanity and its institutions determine whether we eat or die. The increase of political control over physical resources and new technologies only increases the likelihood of famine.

Intergenerational Equity

Capitalism is ultimately attacked on grounds of unsustainability for its purported failure to safeguard the needs of future generations. Without political intervention, it is argued, capitalists would leave a barren globe for their children. Thus, it is concluded, intergenerational equity demands that politics intervene. But are these criticisms valid?

Capitalists care about the future because they care about today's bottom line. Market economies have created major institutions—bond and stock markets, for example—which respond to changes in operating policies that impact future values. A firm that misuses capital or lowers quality standards, a pet store that mistreats its stock, a mine that reduces maintenance, a farmer that permits erosion—all will find the value of their capital assets falling. Highly specialized researchers expend vast efforts ferreting out changes in management practices that might affect future values; investment houses pay future-analysts very well indeed to examine such questions.

Markets, of course, are not able to foresee all eventualities, nor do they consider consequences hundreds of years into the future. Yet, consider the time horizon of politicians. In the United States, at least, they are concerned with only one thing: getting re-elected, a process that provides them at best a two-to-six-year time horizon. Politically-managed infrastructure is routinely undermaintained; funds for new roads are more attractive than the smaller sums used to repair potholes; national forests are more poorly maintained than private forests; erosion is more serious on politically-controlled lands than on those maintained by private corporations. If the free market is shortsighted in its view of the future, then the political process is even more so. It is therefore the free market which best ensures that there will be enough for the future.

Warring Paradigms

The two alternative perspectives on environmental policy— free markets and central planning—differ dramatically. One relies upon individual ingenuity and economic liberty to harness the progressive nature of market forces. The other rests upon political manipulation and government coercion. In point of fact, these approaches are antithetical. There is little hope of developing a "third way." Yet, there has been little debate on which approach offers the greatest promise in enhancing and protecting environmental concerns. The political approach has been adopted on a wide scale throughout the world, with more failure than success, while efforts to utilize the free-market approach have been few and far between.

Nevertheless, there are numerous cases where private property rights have been used to complement and supplement political environmental strategies. One excellent example is a case in England in the 1950s where a fishing club, the Pride of Derby, was able to sue upstream polluters for trespassing against private property. Even the pollution issuing from an upstream municipality was addressed. This ability to go against politically-preferred polluters rarely exists where environmental resources are politically managed.

At the heart of the division between statist and free market environmentalists is a difference in moral vision. Free market environmentalists envision a world in which man and the environment live in harmony, each benefiting from interaction with the other. The other view, which dominates the environmental establishment, believes in a form of ecological apartheid whereby man and nature must be separated, thus protecting the environment from human influence. From this view rises the impetus to establish wilderness lands where no humans may tread, and a quasi-religious zeal to end all human impact on nature.

Thus, the establishment environmentalists view pollution—human waste—as an evil that must be eliminated. That waste is an inevitable by-product of human existence is of secondary concern. To the environmentalist that endorses this ideology, nothing short of civilization's demise will suffice to protect the earth.

The view that free market environmentalists endorse is somewhat different. Not all waste is pollution, but only that waste which is transferred involuntarily. Thus, it is pollution to dispose of garbage on a neighbor's lawn, but not to store it on one's own property. The voluntary transfer of waste, perhaps from an industrialist to the operator of a landfill or recycling facility, is merely another market transaction.

Conclusion

The United Nations Earth Summit considered an extremely important issue: What steps should be taken to ensure that economic and ecological values are harmonized? Unfortunately, the Earth Summit failed to develop such a program, opting instead to further the flawed arguments for ecological central planning.

The world faces a fateful choice as to how to proceed: by expanding the scope of individual action via a system of expanded private property rights and the legal defenses associated with such rights, or by expanding the power of the state to protect such values directly. In making that choice, we should learn from history. Much of the world is only now emerging from decades of efforts to advance economic welfare via centralized political means, to improve the welfare of mankind by restricting economic freedom, by expanding the power of the state, to test out the theory that market forces are inadequate to protect the welfare of society. That experiment has been a clear failure on economic, civil liberties, and even ecological grounds. Economic central planning was a utopian dream; it became a real world nightmare.

Today, the international environmental establishment seems eager to repeat this experiment in the ecological sphere, increasing the power of the state, restricting individual freedom, certain that market forces cannot adequately protect the ecology. Yet, as I've quickly sketched out here, this argument is faulty. Wherever resources have been privately protected, they have done better than their politically managed counterparts—whether we are speaking of elephants in Zimbabwe, salmon streams in England, or beaver in Canada. Where such rights have been absent or suppressed, the results have been less fortunate. Extending property rights to the full array of resources now left undefended, now left as orphans in a world of protected properties, is a daunting challenge. Creative legal arrangements and new technologies will be necessary to protect the oceans and airsheds of the world, but those tasks can be resolved if we apply ourselves. The obstacles to ecological central planning are insurmountable. The need for centralized information and a comprehensive system of controls in order to coerce the population of the world to act in highly restricted ways, as well as that for omniscient decision-makers to choose among technologies, can never be met.

Fred L. Smith, Jr.

Ecological central planning cannot protect the environment, but it can destroy our civil and economic liberties. There is too much at stake to allow the world to embark upon this course. The environment can be protected, and the world's peoples can continue to reach new heights of prosperity, but it is essential to realize that political management is not the proper approach. Rather, the leaders of the world should follow the path of the emerging nations of Eastern Europe and embrace political and economic freedom. In the final analysis, the free market is the only system of truly sustainable development.

Markets and the Environment
A Critical Reappraisal

Fred L. Smith, Jr.

The nature of the environmental problem perhaps is best addressed by reviewing the economic problem. The basic economic problem is scarcity. Demands are unlimited while resources are limited. Most individuals live on a fixed budget; they cannot buy everything they want. Therefore, they must make trade-offs. By eating out, an individual may forgo seeing a movie, or worse, lack sufficient bus fare for work the next morning. Most people would prefer eating out, going to a movie, having bus fare, owning their favorite car, and living in a mansion. However, limited resources prevent meeting all desires. As an individual's resources increase so will the demands upon those resources. The economic problem is never solved.

The environmental problem is no different from the economic problem. Our demand for environmental amenities is unlimited. We want no air pollution, no water pollution, no net loss of wetlands, no net loss of species, no global warming, no acid rain, no ozone depletion, and no risk. We want to live in a beautiful, pristine, and safe environment. However, our resources are limited. The costs of reaching preindustrial levels of air pollution (a goal of the Rio Earth Summit) are prohibitively high. Environmental groups' current campaign to ban chlorine would be extremely costly since chlorine exists in nearly 60 percent of all commercial chemicals

Originally appeared in *Contemporary Economic Policy*, vol. 13, January 1995.
Reproduced by permission of Oxford University Press.

Fred L. Smith, Jr.

(Fumento, 1994). The Delaney Amendment to the Pure Food, Drug, and Cosmetic Act mandated a zero-tolerance level for carcinogens in foods (Simon, 1990). Achieving such levels of purity is too costly to be possible.

Once we recognize our inability to satisfy all of our ecological demands, how do we decide which demands we will satisfy? Which is more important, African elephants or the ozone layer, recycling or population control, reducing carcinogens or increasing fuel efficiency? Is constructing a hierarchy of environmental values possible in a country of 250 million people or a world of five billion? Of course not. People of the African countries identify the more pressing environmental problems as "disease, soil erosion, loss of soil nutrients, lack of sewage disposal and contamination of water by human bodily wastes, insufficient facilities for treatment of drinking water, and lack of refrigeration," while people in the developed countries identify "hazardous waste sites, water pollution from industrial wastes, occupational exposure to toxic chemicals, oil spills, and the destruction of the ozone layer" (Shaw, 1994). Clearly, environmental values differ greatly in different situations. Whose values will decide where our resources should be spent?

Once environmental values have been selected, how will we attain them? Should we select a board of environmental commissioners to manage the environment? Perhaps referendums should be used to achieve our ecological goals. We certainly will need a system that will adapt rapidly to new challenges and new priorities. With new situations will arise new values, new problems, and new possible solutions. How will we adjust to new demands? We must consider these questions in order to increase the supply of environmental amenities. Finally, we must realize that the environmental problem, like the economic problem, never will be solved. As environmental quality increases so will our expectations. Our demands will always exceed our ability to satisfy those demands.

This paper argues for greater attention to the environmental problem and concludes that we can increase environmental quality with limited resources through a program that seeks to integrate ecological resources into the economy via ecological privatization.

That is, more of Planet Earth should be someone's backyard. More of the flora and fauna should be someone's garden or someone's pet. As Kenneth Boulding (1966, p. 231) suggested long ago, if the world is to survive, it must in a very general sense become "domesticated," and people must become "gardeners." Trees cannot have standing, but behind every tree might stand a private owner.

This novel property rights approach to environmental policy may entice more environmental economists to address the important environmental questions. The focus on institutional rather than market failures continues the pioneering work of Hayek, Coase, and Demsetz.

The Market Failure Paradigm

Tyler Cowen (1992, p. 3) states,

> The assertion of market failure is probably the most important argument for governmental intervention. At one time or another nearly every sector of the American economy has been branded as a market failure. Such assertions are usually based upon the theory of public goods and externalities.

The dominant view in the environmental policy arena is that only political management offers any hope of addressing the world's environmental problems. Environmental problems result from "market failures." Economic activities negatively impact the environment, but since such effects are "external" to the market they are ignored. Since markets "fail" to consider external impacts, we must rely on political institutions to remedy the situation. This logic requires politically controlling all economic activities that have environmental consequences.

Unfortunately, all economic activities have environmental consequences. Therefore, the theory of market failure implies political control over the entire economy. Is this course necessary? Should we sacrifice the economy to save the environment? Of course not. The mere fact that markets "fail" (or, at least, fall short of our expectations) does not mean that political institutions will succeed. In the real world, all institutions are flawed and prone to error. As the experience of Eastern Europe suggests, the pitfalls of government failure are far greater than those of the market.

Failures in the Political Market

Efficiency Failures. The 40-year European experiment on whether centralized planning or the free market better advances human welfare is finished. Centralized planning plunged the nations of Eastern Europe into the murky abyss of state management and sluggish economic growth. Economic efficiency without economic freedom is impossible.

Yet, today, the world seems prepared to repeat the disaster. Again we are told that individual liberty must be subsumed to the collective good. Again we are told that individual freedom is incompatible with human welfare. This time, however, we are told that we must sacrifice freedom to save Planet Earth.

Environmental concerns are so important they must not be politicized. But that is exactly what we are doing: we seek clean air or water in the same way that the planned economies of Eastern Europe sought to produce wheat and bread. Political experts determined "desired" output levels, bureaucrats developed detailed plans, and the orders were issued to producers. This process is dominant in the environmental field: government determines environmental quality levels, creates detailed plans, and issues orders.

Eastern European nations did produce some wheat, and our environmental protection agencies have achieved some environmental gains. However, the market-failure explanation of pollution suffers from serious empirical problems. If pollution is the result of markets failing to consider environmental values, then the non-market economies of the world should have fewer environmental problems. Czechoslovakia and Hungary, for example, should have fewer environmental problems than do France and Germany. However, market economies have been far more friendly to the environment. Mikhail Bernstam (1991) shows that per dollar of GNP, socialist economies use nearly three times as much energy as market economies. Former East Germany consumed 40 percent more energy per person and more than 3.5 times as much energy per dollar of GNP than did West Germany. North Korea uses 70 percent more energy per capita than does South Korea. Because market economies use resources more efficiently, they meet human needs with less environmental stress. On the other hand, political management fails to engage the citizenry's creative energies. For economic development to continue with the least environmental impact, we must rely on natural market forces, and not on political controls.

Priority Failures. The environmental challenge is to determine goals and priorities, not how to attain them. The problem in the environment is not that we are doing the right things foolishly, but that we are doing far too many foolish things. As the Environmental Protection Agency (EPA) has moved from controlling a handful of major water and air pollutants to controlling hundreds of trace elements its problems have increased. The EPA initially aimed at controlling small, relatively simple problems, such as lead in gasoline. Political controls were clumsy but somewhat effective. Today, however, the EPA seeks to control many trace pollutants and theoretical health risks (several hundred in the latest Clean Air Act). This task is far more complex and far less responsive to political resolution.

The EPA has had difficulties setting priorities. As newspaper headlines shift attention, so does the EPA. Clean water, clean air, acid rain, hazardous waste, noise pollution, endangered species, wetlands, drift nets in the Pacific, smog in Los Angeles, Amazon rain forests, the ozone hole over Antarctica, pesticides, biotechnology, global warming—all have been priorities at one time or another. Policymakers enact laws and regulations without careful analysis, the public conscience is eased, and a new issue captures the headlines. Because of the erratic and inconsistent nature of politics, legislators focus on enacting laws rather than cleaning up the environment.

An internal study entitled *Unfinished Business* shows the EPA has failed to establish environmentally-defensible goals. It found the EPA's ranking of environmental risks irrational and incoherent (US EPA, 1987). The study included two lists: what the EPA wanted to spend money and staff on. Interestingly, the lists were almost exact opposites. The priorities that emerged out of an environmental rating were the reverse of those that emerged from a political rating. The EPA is a political organization and responds to political, not necessarily ecological, incentives.

Marc Landy, Marc Roberts, and Stephen Thomas (1989) find that the Superfund program wasted vast sums of money on cleaning up "hazardous" waste dumps. The EPA ignored evidence that the dumps posed negligible risks. Superfund, however, remains a priority program because it addresses popular fears, provides "free" money to local communities, and contains few objective criteria to discipline spending. These problems increase as the EPA moves into more policy areas.

Political solutions to environmental problems inevitably respond to political rather than ecological concerns. Only when the
two coincide are the programs successful. That rarely happens.
Because environmental issues rouse passionate responses, politicians respond to emotion, not scientific evidence. Too often the
sensational trumps the serious. We focus on parts-per-billion of
theoretically carcinogenic materials rather than on the real threat of
bacterial contamination. In the past, the EPA has spent large sums
of money controlling Alar, asbestos, dioxin, and radon. In each
case, action has taken precedence over scientific evidence. In this
environment, establishing rational priorities has not been easy.

Public Choice Failures. In fact, the EPA has become part
of the problem by aggravating fears rather than promoting science-
based reassurances. The EPA has suppressed information suggesting
that environmental problems are less serious than previously thought.
Examples abound: withholding urban air pollution statistics that
show dramatic improvements until after passage of the Clean Air
Act; blocking the release of the National Acid Precipitation Assessment Project that showed acid rain to be rather benign; refusing to
clarify "carcinogen" dioxin's risks. After all, the EPA serves its
best interest by intensifying irrational fears through disinformation.
This approach is the surest way to increase the budget. An agency
that alleviates fears, thereby diminishing its importance, may face
major cutbacks.

Moreover, government policy is subject to manipulation and
control by special interests. These interests seek private gain at the
public's expense (Greve and Smith, 1992). The US government
now spends nearly $150 billion annually on the environment (US
EPA, 1990). The recent Clean Air Act will increase this figure substantially. Money attracts interests who seek to minimize their costs
or penalize their competitors. As a result, the EPA has become a
major forum for special interest pleading. Alternative fuels, solar

power, electric cars, mass transit, reforestation, and energy conservation all have benefited from federal subsidies.

One of the best examples of political interests running roughshod over environmental concerns is the EPA's ethanol mandate. A coalition made up of environmentalists, the Renewable Fuels Association, the Clean Fuels Development Coalition, the National Corn Growers Association, and the Archer Daniels Midland Company, which is the largest domestic producer of ethanol and the only company with both Republican and Democratic backing, achieved a *de facto* ethanol mandate by acquiring a minimum-oxygen requirement that was possible only with an ethanol mixture. However, ethanol is hardly an environmentally-benign fuel (Adler, 1992).

Pork barrels are easier to fill if painted green. The EPA's recent ethanol decision shows that political moonshine remains very potable in Washington. Political pariahs (e.g. the oil and automobile industries) are hit hard, while the politically preferred (e.g. farmers, environmentalists, and alternative fuel interests) are treated lightly and preferentially. The ethanol incident demonstrates

> that legislators were prepared to go to extraordinary lengths in creating a market for ethanol, regardless of the environmental results. The result is a regulatory regime of mind-boggling complexity, a web of standards, mandates, requirements, and timetables that is incomprehensible to all but a handful of bureaucrats and to representatives of the interests that are being regulated or served. (Adler, 1992, p. 39)

The Myth of Public Participation

Public participation encourages specific "publics" or interests to get involved. Most of us are too busy to learn about the many political issues and to understand all of the scientific, political, and economic implications of government policy. As a result, only those groups who are motivated by economic or ideological interests participate in the process. Bruce Yandle (1983) describes such political coalitions as "Bootleggers and Baptists" and notes that they are found in almost all policy struggles.

Because of the knowledge gap between the public and those motivated by necessity to be informed, bureaucrats and special interests are able to misuse or ignore scientific and economic evidence to advance their agenda. The acid rain issue is a good example. Acid rain was believed to be the cause of dying forests in much of the United States and Canada. Congress commissioned a 10-year, $570 million study to evaluate its effects. The National Acid Precipitation Assessment Program, as it was titled, found "there is no evidence of widespread forest damage from current ambient levels of acidic rain in the United States." Congress, the President, and the EPA ignored the study and passed an acid rain program anyway. The program will cost between $3 and $7 billion and will lead to more than 200,000 lost jobs (Adler, 1992, p. 41). We're spending lots of green dollars, but we're getting few green results.

Other programs have also been completely ineffective and often unnecessary. Superfund, a waste-site cleanup program created after toxic waste was discovered beneath the community of Love Canal, New York, is the epitome of bad science and political pork. Every state was guaranteed a cleanup site regardless of the EPA's risk assessment ranking. The risk assessment criteria are fantastically overcautious. It is assumed that children will be present, will live at the site for 70 years, ingest approximately a teaspoonfull of dirt a day, and will only use contaminated ground water for bathing and drinking (Jeffreys, 1994). The two most famous (or infamous) Superfund sites, Times Beach and Love Canal, were both evacuated and cleaned up at enormous cost. Later, the EPA admitted that the risks posed were nearly zero and did not justify the actions taken. However, Superfund now has a life of its own and continues to expand in spite of its dismal record.

In sum, the effort to control pollution politically is encountering many problems. Costs are high, while success is limited. Priorities are irrational and inconsistent. Special interest groups are becoming more adept at steering policy to advance their own interests. None of this leads to effective environmental policy for the United States.

Backlash

The failures of environmental policy are creating an opportunity for reform. The costs of current policies are becoming evident. The easy "haystack" problems have been solved, the political pariahs have been purged. The remaining "needle in the haystack" problems are now impacting politically preferred polluters. As Rick Henderson (1994, p. 50) says,

> Environmental regulations have reached beyond factory smokestacks and corporate dumpers. Now they can prevent a congregation of 120 Baptists in Florida from building a church and a retired couple in Michigan from constructing a home on a lakefront lot they've owned for 25 years.

The EPA's need to expand its power is affecting larger segments of society, and this is beginning to have political repercussions.

Environmental policies have blocked economic growth in communities and in some cases whole regions of the United States. The Endangered Species Act has closed off millions of acres of timberland, depriving thousands of Pacific Northwestern families of their livelihood. It has also been used to divest property owners of the use of their land. Superfund has transformed former industrial regions into nondevelopment zones, known as "brownfields." Bill Ellen, a marine and environmental consultant, was overseeing the construction of wetlands which would serve as a hunting and conservation preserve. However, he was arrested and sent to jail for six months for destroying wetlands. His crime was dumping two truckloads of dirt on dry land (Orient, 1993).

Criticism has led to a growing interest in reform. Most of the debate is focused on the introduction of "market mechanisms," i.e., regulatory taxes or quotas. Environmental goals will still be set politically, but market forces will be harnessed to achieve efficiency. "Market mechanisms," we are told, offer a "third way" between political controls and free markets. The options of this third way include pollution taxes (eco-taxes), tradable emission rights (eco-quotas), deposit systems, full cost pricing, Demand-Side Management, user fees, and so forth.

The Case Against "Market Mechanisms"

Ludwig von Mises (1949, pp. 706-707) clearly stated why the advocates of market mechanisms are deluded. He said,

> What these neosocialists suggest is really paradoxical. They want to abolish private control of the means of production, market exchange, market prices, and competition. But at the same time they want to organize the socialist utopia in such a way that people could act as if these things were still present. They want people to play market as children play war, railroad, or school. They do not comprehend how such childish play differs from the real thing it tries to imitate.

In other words, it is foolish to believe that the incentives present in the market can be duplicated in the absence of property rights. People will not act as if they are property owners if they don't own property. Without something to sell and without the possibility of personal gain, market signals have no relevance; they are ignored. Anthony de Jasay (1990, p. 16) stated that the "socialist countries that tried to abandon the command economy without also re-defining and de-centralizing property rights...found themselves with an economy that heeded no signals of any sort." Does market socialism as outlined by socialists like Lange, Lerner, Leiberman, Le Grand, and Estrin, or as attempted in Yugoslavia, relate to tradable quota systems and other market-based policies? The author thinks it does.

What are the problems with Tradable Emission Allowance Systems (TEAS)? First, TEAS, like other market socialist experiments, do not adequately define property rights. For a property right to exist it must be securely defined and guaranteed. If it is not, then an actor in the market will not respond to market signals. In the case of TEAS, property rights are not secure. Permits are issued by law and, therefore, can be expropriated by law. The property right is as unstable as the mood of the American electorate.

Second, government can re- or de-value the permits. After a baseline (the amount of pollution allowed) is set, Congress may decide that its estimate was wrong. It may be thought that there is still too much pollution or that its baseline is too stringent. If pollution is still considered too high, then the number of permits will be reduced and companies will lose part of their pollution quota. If the baseline is considered too low then additional permits will be issued, decreasing their value and hurting the holders of permits. If government left the baseline alone, property rights might be considered secure and the system may work. However, if government insists on tinkering—and government can never resist tinkering—then uncertainty is introduced. Those operating in the "market" will not respond to market signals because property rights are insecure or nonexistent.

This brings us to another problem. For property rights to be secure in a politically-created market we would have to live in a static world. Once the "optimal"—a word freely tossed about by advocates of market-based policies—baseline was discovered there would be no need for change and security could be achieved. However, it would be impossible to determine the "optimal" baseline in the real world where dynamic and uncontrollable forces are always at work. Even if it were possible to discover all of the necessary information (i.e., people's values, amounts of pollution produced, geological and climatological forces, available technologies, available resources, etc., etc., etc.), make all the calculations, and implement the results politically, it wouldn't matter. By the time policy was set in motion conditions would have changed and the information would be irrelevant.

This, of course, is the fundamental flaw in all socialist schemes, as shown by F.A. Hayek (1945). Socialist planners of all shades, both red and green, have failed to overcome this problem. Frances Cairncross (1992, p. 100), one of the foremost advocates of market-based policies, acknowledges this problem:

> It is almost impossible to set them [pollution taxes] at the "right" level. That magic point, at which the costs of pollution prevention catch up with the benefits, is hard enough to discover even on paper. To hit it by setting taxes at precisely the right level is even more difficult. Keeping taxes at that right level, year after year, is probably impossible.

The same, of course, holds true for setting a baseline for TEAS.

Finally, pollution permits erect barriers of entry into the market. New companies may be restricted from entering the market because there are no available permits to allow industry expansion. Also, existing companies with surplus permits will not likely sell to potential competitors. Essentially, TEAS introduce anti-competitive dynamics into the market which shield older, inefficient companies from competition by new, innovative, and more efficient companies. In the long run, protecting existing companies may mean more pollution. Stifling competition does not allow for the "survival of the fittest" (i.e., survival of the most efficient and least polluting). Politically-created markets effectively crowd out other market forces which achieve, without intention, pollution reduction. Timothy Wirth (Wirth and Heinz, 1988 and 1990), the former Colorado Democrat who introduced Project-88, a tradable emission quota system, stated, "This report is an attempt to put a 'green thumb' on Adam Smith's invisible hand." However, there is no need to put a green thumb on the invisible hand. It already has one.

The "Right" to Pollute vs. The Common Law

Environmentalists argue that TEAS create a right to pollute. Many environmentalists view pollution as a sin and are offended by this newly concocted and politically enforced right. Economists dismiss this argument, but the author believes it has great validity, not because pollution is a sin but because issuing a right to pollute to one violates the property rights of another. An important distinction should be made when discussing pollution. Waste or an emission cannot be considered pollution until it travels onto another's property or causes nuisance to another person. As long as a person or company internalizes waste by disposing of it on their own property or paying another for waste disposal rights, pollution does not occur. Only when waste is dumped without permission on another's property can it be called pollution.

In truth, all types of environmental policy, both command-and-control and market-based policies, legalize pollution. The common law maxim, "so use your own property as not to injure the property of another," has been corrupted, through current legislation, to allow legally permissible amounts of pollution. Individuals are deprived legal recourse against property damage. Under common law, property rights reign supreme. One cannot dispose of waste on another's property without their permission. If one does so they can sue for redress. Under our current system the government sanctions politically-determined levels of pollution. Since pollution to a certain level is legal it is no longer actionable. Market-based policies infringe upon property rights and ignore the most effective means of pollution control (Meiners and Yandle, 1992).

Finally, the serious problems already discussed which plague the EPA would remain under a system of market-based policies. Market-based policies are essentially designed to induce companies to reduce pollution in a more efficient and cost effective manner. However, they do nothing to address the political problems inherent in government-determined environmental quality. The "optimal" amount of pollution is still determined through policy mechanisms (i.e., quotas and taxes). Priorities are still set politically. The inability of the EPA to set rational goals will not be corrected. The incentives at the EPA to misuse science and fan the fears of the populace will continue. In short, the entire irrational and perverse incentive system which exists at the EPA will remain intact. Genuine environmental problems will continue to be overlooked, while the sensational will capture the headlines and influence policy.

Free Market Environmentalism

The fundamental conflict over who controls the use of our air, water, and landscape cannot be decided merely through a change in the instruments of enforcement. We must be willing to change the institutions by which these conflicts are solved. As discussed, environmental problems are a dynamic and intricate puzzle. Central planners, even if altruistic and immune to politics, cannot accumulate the necessary information which will lead to the correct solutions. Because central planners are not immune to political influence, their inability together with perverse incentives leads to disastrous environmental consequences. There must be a better way. Fortunately, there is. Markets provide a means of solving the knowledge problem, and property rights establish the proper incentives necessary to care for the environment, thereby satisfying our demands for environmental amenities. Speaking of the knowledge problem and the solutions to that problem, Israel M. Kirzner (1984, p. 416) states,

> [The] entrepreneurial element in human action is what responds to the signals for pure profit that are generated by the errors that arise out of the dispersed knowledge available in society. It is this yeast that ferments the competitive-entrepreneurial discovery process, tending to reveal to market participants more and more of the relevant information scattered throughout the market. It is this entrepreneurial-competitive process that thus grapples with that basic knowledge problem we found inescapably to confront central planning authorities. To the extent that central planning displaces the entrepreneurial discovery process, whether on the society-wide scale of comprehensive planning or on the more modest scale of state piecemeal intervention in an otherwise free market, the planners are at the same time both smothering the market's ability to transcend the basic knowledge problem and subjecting themselves helplessly to that very problem. The problem's source is Hayek's dispersed knowledge: Central planning has no tools with which to engage the problem of dispersed knowledge, and its very centralization means that the market's discovery process has been impeded, if not brought to a full halt.

By allowing the market free rein, the knowledge problem is solved. By securing property rights, the proper incentives will be instilled. The owner of environmental amenities will employ those amenities, first, so as not to infringe on others rights and, second, to satisfy the demands of potential users of the amenity. Whatever the decided use, owners would be foolish to wantonly destroy or waste the resource for short-term profit. Rather, it is in their interest to cultivate, conserve, and renew the resource for future income. This is the definition of good stewardship and the only way to achieve "sustainable development."

Let me illustrate with an example from Canada's history as documented by Harold Demsetz (1967). In pre-colonial times beaver were plentiful throughout the territory that would become Canada. Native American demands upon the beaver were low, and therefore represented little threat to the beaver population. However, this did not last. When French fur trappers arrived, conditions changed. High demand for beaver pelts in Europe along with French technologies, such as guns and traps, greatly improved hunting efficiency, and had serious effects. Trapping expanded rapidly, resulting in a sharp decline in the beaver population.

The indigenous populations were aware of this problem and met to resolve the issue. Traditionally, beaver had been common property—any beaver could be taken by any man. That system worked well while demand was low and supply high. However, the arrival of Europeans made the system unsustainable. To meet increased demand while preserving the beaver, the Indians instituted property rights by giving each family group an area containing at least one beaver lodge. In effect, beavers were privatized. Rules for dispute settlement and policing procedures also evolved. Families that overexploited their resource immediately suffered the economic consequences, while those that used their beavers wisely prospered. Property rights ensured sustainability and restored the balance between Man and beaver—a balance that survived until the English arrived and the property rights system collapsed. After that, beavers were hunted to near extinction.

This story suggests private stewardship of environmental resources is a powerful means of ensuring sustainability. The best way to preserve the environment is through ecological privatization. By doing this we implement a method through which environmental priorities can emerge in a sensible and rational manner.

The evolutionary manner in which property rights emerged among the northern American Indian tribes illustrates an important point. Before beaver pelts became valuable as a commodity in Europe, the common property system worked well. The relatively low human population together with the low value of beaver as a food or clothing source meant that the externalities present in a common property system were small enough to negate the need for property rights. In other words, the fact that any beaver could be taken by any man at any time posed no threat to the survival of the beaver. With the increased value of beaver pelts and the arrival of more people with better technology, externality costs were raised to where they exceeded the cost of implementing and enforcing property rights. Ecological privatization became necessary to internalize the externality and to preserve the existence of the beaver for both current and future profit opportunities.

The establishment of property rights gives incentives to use resources in a sustainable fashion. On the other hand, through the exchange process, resources will rise to their most highly valued use. If a resource becomes scarce the price will rise and demand will decrease. Furthermore, substitutes will be sought in order to satisfy the demand for that resource function. Many times the substitute will be better than the original. Without the exchange mechanism and property rights we are left with a system of "groping about in the dark," as Mises puts it.

The case for free market environmentalism is rather simple for those resources in which property rights are easily defined and exchanged. However, there are more difficult environmental areas where defining property rights appears to be impossible. As one critic, Robert Stavins (1989, p. 96) asked, "Does anyone really believe that acid rain can be efficiently controlled by assigning private property rights for the US airshed and then effecting negotiations among all affected parties?" Certainly it is one thing to put a fence around one's land, or to patrol it to deter poachers, litterers, and other undesirables. It is quite another to keep unauthorized fishing boats out of one's stretch of ocean or to identify the source of pollution that is damaging one's orchard (or lungs).

How do we "fence" the airshed, ground water, or the oceans? This feat appears as difficult to us now as did the fencing of the Western frontier in the 19th century. In those windswept, arid plains, substantial acreage was needed to sustain a family, and building wooden fences or stone walls to "privatize" land was prohibitively expensive. An 1850s Stavins would have argued that in such a situation no property rights solution was feasible, just as the real Stavins does today with regard to air and water. Yet the problem of property rights in the West was resolved through voluntary actions. Institutions evolved which defined and protected property rights. Ultimately a technology—barbed wire—greatly reduced the costs of marking property boundaries (Anderson and Hill, 1975).

Technologies now exist that make it possible to determine, within limits, the quantity and types of air pollution entering a region. Lasimetrics, for example, can map atmospheric chemical concentrations from orbit. In time, that science might provide a sophisticated means of tracking cross-boundary pollution flows. Also, large installations such as power plants could add (or be required to add) chemical or isotopic "labels" to their emissions to facilitate tracking. Such "labeling" has long been routine in the manufacture of explosives, to help trace explosives used in crime or terrorism.

If not perfect, the market is the best solution to our ecological problems. Only under a system where resources are privately held will people have the ability to accurately express their environmental values. Only through a price system will those values be conveyed to entrepreneurs who can in turn satisfy those values.

Conclusion

The focus on "economic instruments" is misguided; tools *per se* do not improve anything—the guillotine did not make France a more just society. Instead we need to focus on institutions. Through comparative institutional analysis of different schemes for wildlife protection and other ecological resource management we can discover better solutions (see Simmons and Krueter, 1989; Jeffreys, 1991; Smith, 1988; Leal, 1993; Adler, 1993).

Such studies could be carried out in other areas to determine the appropriate means to protect resources. For example, we should compare the rates of technological change in resource management in both the free market and in the politically-managed environment. Interdisciplinary research such as economic analysis of traditional societal management regimes (cultural anthropology remedies) might be valuable (Cordell, 1989). Current legal and other impediments (uniform national standards, disallowal of ownership, inability to risk contract) that inhibit private stewardship arrangements should be studied. Finally, we need to understand the evolution of the common law, to explore how such traditional property-rights defenses might be restored and strengthened, and to examine the various ways the common law addresses the "many/many problem" (many creators of a cost, many parties impacted by that cost). For example, privatized highways would make owners of the highway liable for emission levels; the owner would decide how to allocate such costs to road users. Neighborhood associations might determine what level of air quality would be sought and bargain accordingly (Anderson and Leal, 1991). Malls decide what level of amenity their customers will be afforded; mall customers "consume" air conditioning and other "public goods." Generally such costs are paid indirectly via surcharges to the various tenants. If costs mount, common spaces may shrink, common amenities may be scaled back.

Let me end with a comment by Ronald Coase. In his book, *The Firm, the Market, and the Law* (1988), he mentions his criticism of neoclassical economists has not been well understood—specifically his criticism of the Pigouvian tax. Even Baumol, a friend, didn't quite get it. Baumol argued the logic of a tax-and-subsidy system as discussed by Coase is "impeccable." However, we do not know how to calculate such taxes and subsidies or how to approximate them by trial and error. "This I have never denied," replies Coase. "My point was simply that such tax proposals are the stuff that dreams are made of. In my youth is was said that what was too silly to be said may be sung. In modern economics it may be put into mathematics" (Coase, 1988, p. 185).

It's time to stop being silly and start thinking seriously about what we might do to improve the planet on which we live.

References

Adler, Jonathan H., "Clean Fuels, Dirty Air," in *Environmental Politics: Public Costs, Private Rewards*, Michael S. Greve and Fred L. Smith, Jr., eds. (New York: Praeger, 1992), pp. 19-49.

Adler, Jonathan H., "Poplar Front: The Rebirth of America's Forests," *Policy Review* (Spring 1993), pp. 84-87 [see pp. 65-75 in this volume].

Anderson, Terry L., and P.J. Hill, "The Evolution of Property Rights: A Study of the American West," *Journal of Law and Economics*, vol. 12 (1975), pp. 163-179.

Anderson, Terry L., and Donald R. Leal, *Free Market Environmentalism* (Boulder, Colorado: Westview Press, 1991).

Bernstam, Mikhail, *The Wealth of Nations and the Environment* (London: Institute of Economic Affairs, 1991).

Fred L. Smith, Jr.

Boulding, Kenneth E., "Economics and Ecology," *Future Environments of North America*, F. Fraser Darling and John P. Milton, eds. (Garden City, New York: The Natural History Press, 1966), pp. 225-234.

Cairncross, Frances, *Costing the Earth: The Challenge for Governments, the Opportunities for Business*, (Boston: Harvard Business School, 1992).

Coase, R.H., *The Firm, the Market, and the Law* (Chicago: The University of Chicago Press, 1988).

Cordell, John, *A Sea of Small Boats* (Cambridge, Massachusetts: Cultural Survival, Inc., 1989).

Cowen, Tyler, *Public Goods and Market Failures* (New Brunswick, New Jersey: Transaction Publishers, 1992).

Demsetz, Harold, "Toward a Theory of Property Rights," *American Economic Review* (May 1967), pp. 347-60.

Fumento, Michael, "Chemical Warfare," *Reason* (June 1994), pp. 42-43.

Greve, Michael S., and Fred L. Smith, Jr., eds., *Environmental Politics: Public Costs, Private Rewards* (New York: Praeger, 1992).

Hayek, Friedrich A., "The Use of Knowledge in Society," *American Economic Review* (September 1945), pp. 519-530.

Henderson, Rick, "Bill Killers," *Reason* (August/September 1994), pp. 50-52.

de Jasay, Anthony, *Market Socialism: A Scrutiny, 'This Square Circle'* (London: Institute of Economic Affairs, 1990).

Jeffreys, Kent, *Reinventing Superfund: The Clinton Reform Proposal and an Alternative* (Washington, DC: Competitive Enterprise Institute, 1994).

Jeffreys, Kent, *Who Should Own the Ocean?* (Washington, DC: Competitive Enterprise Institute, 1991).

Kirzner, Israel M., "Economic Planning and the Knowledge Problem," *Cato Journal* (Fall 1984), pp. 407-18.

Landy, Marc K., Marc J. Roberts, and Stephen R. Thomas, *The Environmental Protection Agency: Asking the Wrong Questions* (Oxford: Oxford University Press, 1989).

Leal, Donald R., *Receipts and Costs of Logging on Government Forests: A Federal and State Comparison in Montana* (Bozeman, Montana: Political Economy Research Center, 1993).

Meiners, Roger E., and Bruce Yandle, *The Common Law Solution to Water Pollution: The Path Not Taken* (Bozeman, Montana: Political Economy Research Center, 1992).

von Mises, Ludwig, *Human Action: A Treatise on Economics* (Chicago: Henry Regnery Company, 1949).

Orient, Jane M., "Eco-Justice," *The Freeman* (September 1993), p. 357.

Shaw, Jane S., "Things Are Better Than We Think (And Could be Better Yet)," *The Freeman* (June 1994), pp. 276-78.

Simmons, Randy, and Urs Krueter, "Herd Mentality: Banning Ivory Sales Is No Way to Save the Elephant," *Policy Review* (Fall 1989), pp. 46-49 [see pp. 111-121 in this volume].

Simon, Julian, *Population Matters* (New Brunswick, New Jersey: Transaction Publishers, 1990).

Smith, Robert J., "Private Solutions to Conservation Problems," in *The Theory of Market Failure: A Critical Examination*, Tyler Cowen, ed. (Fairfax, Virginia: George Mason University Press, 1988).

Stavins, Robert, A letter printed in *Policy Review* (Summer 1989), pp. 95-96.

US EPA, *Environmental Investments: The Cost of a Clean Environment*, Science, Economics, and Statistics Division (Washington, DC: Office of Regulatory Management and Evaluation; Office of Policy, Planning and Evaluation, 1990).

US EPA, *Unfinished Business: A Comparative Assessment of Environmental Problems* (Washington, DC: Office of Policy Analysis, 1987).

Fred L. Smith, Jr.

Wirth, Senator Timothy E., and Senator John Heinz, Sponsors, *Project 88— Round I & Round II* (Washington, DC: 1988 and 1990).

Yandle, Bruce, "Bootleggers and Baptists—The Education of a Regulatory Economist," *Regulation* (May/June 1983), pp. 12-16.

❖❖ **Natural Resources**

Poplar Front
The Rebirth of America's Forests

Jonathan H. Adler

At the turn of the century, leaders in the emerging conservation movement warned that the United States would soon run out of trees. President Theodore Roosevelt observed, "If the present rate of forest destruction is allowed to continue, with nothing to offset it, a timber famine in the future is inevitable." Gifford Pinchot, the father of the United States Forest Service, was another pessimist: "The United States has already crossed the verge of a timber famine so severe that its blighting effects will be felt by every household in the land."

These forecasts of a timber shortage were not without foundation. The 19th and early-20th centuries saw the deforestation of vast tracts of land. By 1920, only 600 million of America's previous 1 billion acres of forest remained. The demand for cropland, building materials, and fuelwood had taken its toll on forests. Between 1850 and 1920, fuelwood consumption tripled, and industrial wood consumption quintupled. Rising population threatened to put further pressure on forests as wood was used for everything from homes and fences to railroad ties.

Many areas that once held rich, expansive forests largely were depleted of trees. It has been said when the first European settlers arrived, a squirrel could travel from Maine to the Mississippi River without touching the ground. But during the 19th

---

A shorter version of this essay appeared in *Policy Review*, Spring 1993. Reprinted with permission.

century, much of the eastern United States was cleared for farm-land. At one point, according to Forest Service Assistant Director Douglas MacCleery, farmers were clearing forests at the amazing clip of 8,640 acres per day, a rate that continued for over 50 years. As Roger Sedjo of Resources for the Future noted in *America's Renewable Resources*, "Not only had the area in forestland reached its historic low in 1920, but much of the forest that remained in the East was low-quality, low-volume, degraded forest, often used for grazing."

230 Billion Trees

In the past 70 years American forests have been reborn. The area of forestland is about the same: 600 million acres in the lower 48 states, or just under one-third of total land mass; 730 million acres with Alaska and Hawaii. But America has more trees, 230 billion now, because there is greater tree-density per acre. Indeed, there are more standing trees in America today than at any point in this century.

Particularly notable has been the resurgence of forests east of the Mississippi, where reforestation has been the rule rather than the exception. In the past 40 years, timberland east of the Mississippi has expanded by 3.8 million acres, in addition to the nearly three million acres in the eastern United States that have been declared wilderness in the past two decades. By 1980, New England contained more forested acres than in the mid-19th century; Vermont is now twice as forested as then. Fifty-nine percent of the northeastern United States is covered by forest, a particularly remarkable fact since the Northeast's population density, at 260 people per square mile, is over three times the national average. Today the southern United States is responsible for nearly half of the net annual forest growth in America—some 10 billion cubic feet—while also providing over half of the harvested volume of timber. Pinchot and Roosevelt hardly would have believed this was possible.

Appalachian Spring

This huge forest growth occurred largely because farmers left the eastern United States in favor of more fertile lands in the Midwest, allowing for tremendous reforestation in the East. Many areas that now house thriving forests once were cleared for logging or agricultural purposes. The Shenandoah National Park, one of the most popular in the entire national park system, was once rough, relatively unproductive farm land. Hilton Head, a South Carolina island resort known for its lush surroundings of oaks and palmettos, was cleared for agriculture before the Civil War. Beginning at the turn of the century, the island was managed by private owners for timber and wildlife, allowing the forest to grow back. Moreover, the Eastern Wilderness Act of 1974 established many areas as "wilderness"—defined as a tract or region uncultivated and uninhabited by human being"—that had previously been cleared, some within the past 60 years. This is even true of the Boundary Waters wilderness area in Minnesota, considered by many to be the premier wilderness area in the eastern United States.

In 1885, two-thirds of the original forest in the Adirondacks had been logged at least once. At that time, much of the land was made a New York state preserve to be kept as "wild forest lands." Today, there is talk of creating additional wilderness in Adirondack lands that had once been cleared for logging and subsistence farming. Earlier clearing of these lands has not prevented the return of the natural forest ecosystems.

Forest regeneration in the western United States has been less dramatic than in the East. Nonetheless, even the West is experiencing net forest growth. Although some western states, such as Oregon and Washington, recently have been plagued with political conflicts over forest-management practices, forest planting in these states has increased over 50 percent in the past 20 years. In 1990, the United States Forest Service reported that Oregon and Washington ranked fifth and sixth in the nation in the number of acres planted.

The United States has approximately 900 trees for every American. And as American forests have grown more healthy and robust, they have provided more timber output. The standing volume of trees in America's forests is now 24 percent higher than just 40 years ago. Led by increases in hardwood forest inventories, timber growth has risen nearly 70 percent per acre since 1952. There are three major reasons for the improvement in America's forests: 1) the development of better forest management techniques such as wildfire control; 2) rapid technological change that has reduced per capita timber demand; and 3) price signals that have given private landowners an incentive to plant trees.

Taming Wildfire

Wildfire, both natural and man-made, devastated forests in the 19th and early-20th centuries. These fires whipped across forested expanses, consuming tens of thousands of acres at a time. At the turn of the century, forest fires consumed as many as 50 million acres annually—an area as great as West Virginia, Virginia, and Maryland combined—and were responsible for hundreds of deaths. No wonder fire suppression became a major focus of the United States Forest Service (USFS) in the 1920s.

Because of its massive impact on forests, controlling wildfire has been one of the most important developments in encouraging the growth of America's timber industry. Today, wildfire rarely consumes one-tenth of its turn-of-the-century highs. While 1872 typically is remembered as the year of the Chicago fire, that same year a forest fire killed some 1,500 people and consumed one million acres of trees near Peshtigo, Wisconsin. Such disasters largely are a thing of the past thanks to fire-management efforts.

Forest fires, of course, often clear the way for forest regeneration. By clearing the land of older stands, fires enable younger trees to grow, particularly those that are shade intolerant and are unable to grow under the forest canopy. Some tree species, particularly certain species of pine, thrive as a result of smaller forest fires that eliminate competition from less-resistant species. Nonetheless, forest fires can decimate regions and destroy habitat. Controlling these outbreaks has allowed the development of healthier forest ecosystems in many areas, as has the use of prescribed burning.

The prospect of uncontrolled fires has been a major disincentive to the planting of new trees. Private land owners, although enticed by the prospect of profiting from the harvest of timber, were discouraged by the prospect of having their investment destroyed by wildfire. As a result, before fire suppression rose to prominence after World War II, tree planting remained under 200,000 acres annually. By 1970, annual tree planting covered over 1.5 million acres, and today almost three million acres are planted. Most planting has occurred on private lands, and it is certain that much of it would not have occurred if private landowners had to worry about the threat of wildfire.

How Cars Save Trees

As improved fire-control techniques raised incentives to plant trees, rapid technological changes led to more efficient use of forest resources. The development of wood preservatives, for example, has lengthened the life-span of timber products such as railroad ties, which once composed over 20 percent of annual timber use. By 1960, railroads accounted for only 5 to 6 percent of timber consumption, as few new lines were being built and few ties had to be replaced.

The rise of the automobile spared millions of acres of forest. Rural communities no longer had to depend on rail transportation, with its enormous wood requirements. Autos also reduced the pressure to convert forest into farmland. This is because the acreage devoted to feeding draft animals—one-quarter of all cropland at the turn of the century—could decline sharply as autos replaced horse-drawn carriages and tractors replaced animal-drawn farm equipment.

The spectacular advances in farm productivity resulting from chemical fertilizers and pesticides, hybrid seed varieties, and farm machinery also limited the need for cropland acreage, even as America's population continued to rise. Average corn yields per acre, for example, have more than tripled since 1935. This has left more room for oak, hickory, and pine.

Today the oil and gas industry also protects North America from the kind of deforestation now occurring in much of the developing world. In 1850, the United States used approximately 50 percent of harvested timber as fuelwood, and firewood provided over 90 percent of the Btus (British Thermal Units) produced. Today, only 20 percent of wood consumption is fuelwood, as fossil fuels have largely displaced wood as an energy source for heating and cooking. By contrast, over half of the timber harvested in the rest of the world is used for fuel, and in lesser-developed nations the portion of timber consumed for fuel is 80 percent.

During this century timber mills have become vastly more efficient in using wood. Thinner sawblades and computer control of sawing have dramatically reduced waste, while the introduction of fiberboard and other wood products has turned what were once wood scraps into marketable products. As with many industries, market pressures have induced profit-seeking firms to develop innovative methods of increasing efficiency and reducing waste. The prospect of an inexpensive source of timber prompted Tree Technology International, Inc., to develop a paulownia clone that matures in seven years—one-sixth the standard for hardwood.

Meanwhile, price signals have given landowners the incentive to increase the timber supply by replanting. Over 80 percent of forest planting—covering approximately three million acres—now occurs on private land each year. As long as there is a substantial demand for timber, these trends likely will continue.

In December 1992, there was even a glut of Christmas trees on the market, resulting in prices as low as $5 per tree. Albert Gondeck, executive director of the Maine Christmas Tree Association, told the Associated Press, "There aren't enough people for all the trees." The glut occurred because so many trees were planted by speculators looking to make a profit.

For some applications, however, entrepreneurs have been driven to develop cheaper timber substitutes. While wood once dominated building construction, today concrete and steel have displaced much timber use. Such substitutions reinforce the general trend toward a more sustainable timber supply, brought about not by government planning, but by market responses to the potential of resource scarcity. As long as timber companies stand to make a profit from forest cultivation, they will replant. This is true even in the wake of natural disasters: When the slopes of Mount St. Helens were consumed by the volcano's eruption in 1980, Weyerhauser promptly planted more than 18 million trees over the following six years.

Public vs. Private

Many would credit the USFS with spearheading the resurgence of America's forests. The Forest Service was founded for that purpose in response to a perceived market failure to protect forest resources. However, it is not clear that the control of vast tracts of land by the federal government was nearly as important as the control of land by private, profit-seeking individuals. The vast majority of tree planting occurs on private land. While public property managers gain little financial benefit from sensible stewardship policies, the private property owner stands to lose or gain based on the quality of his or her management decisions. The same incentives simply do not exist on government-managed lands.

Consider that the National Forests contained 17.6 percent of US timberlands, while accounting for only 15 percent of the nation's annual forest growth on timberland in 1986. That same year almost 20 percent of timberland growth occurred on forest-industry land, which contains less than 15 percent of timberland. In forest growth, the public sector has also lagged behind: "Timber volume increased in the last 10 years for all ownerships except national forests, which had an 8 percent decrease in volume," according to a 1989 Forest Service report.

The lower growth on National Forest land is not the result of uncontrolled harvesting. On the contrary, timber productivity, measured by timber output on forest lands, is lower in the national forests than in private timberlands. USFS lands account for almost 45 percent of America's softwood inventory. Yet these lands have accounted for less than 25 percent of the softwood on the market since 1988. While a private property owner would be sacrificing potential profits from such decisions, the managers of public lands are insulated from the economic costs of their decisions.

Despite the importance of private lands in America's forest resurgence, "private property" is almost a dirty term within the environmental establishment. Leaders from within the movement repeatedly inveigh against private property rights as a destructive force and a relic of the 18th century. University of Illinois law professor Eric Freyogle wrote approvingly in *The New York Times* that "Environmentalism's essential message is that private ownership rights go too far." Senator John Chafee (R-RI) concurred that the environment cannot be adequately protected if policy-makers "give in" to private-property rights.

Yet the institution of private property has been instrumental in fostering greater forest growth and improvement in forest management. Environment Probe, headquartered in Toronto, Ontario, points out that private ownership has tended to produce better timber management practices worldwide. Whereas Pinchot once remarked that "government control of cutting on all timberland, private as well as public," is necessary to ensure an adequate timber supply, many experts now point to government management as part of the problem. It is unlikely that non-forest-industry private lands would have tripled tree planting rates in the last 20 years were it not for the potential economic gain—and it is the institution of private property that makes such gains possible.

Spots of Decline

While overall trends are positive, the state of America's forests is not without blemishes. The Pacific Northwest has seen a modest decline in timber volume per acre, approximately 5 percent in the past four decades. Northwestern forests have declined moderately, in part as a result of selective harvesting of Ponderosa pine that leaves the remaining stands more vulnerable to insect infestation, and in part as a result of regulatory policies which encourage the acceleration of timber cutting rotations. In the East, the population of black walnut has declined sharply as a result of heavy harvesting and only modest regrowth, although the number of black walnut tree farms is rising.

Some other popular species of trees have been ravaged by disease and pests. Gypsy moths, Dutch elm disease, and white pine blister rust have taken a terrible toll. The majestic American chestnut, once the primary hardwood in eastern forests, was virtually wiped out by a blight from Europe that arrived at the turn of the century. Growing insect and disease infestation is raising concern about the health of forests in eastern Oregon's Blue Mountains.

In spite of these problems, there is hope for some of the threatened species. Fusiform rust has attacked several species of southern pines, including the loblolly. Timber companies and forest officials have responded by interbreeding resistant strains of these species and developing resistant nursery stock to promote some recovery. Similar efforts have been undertaken to combat white pine blister rust. There is also the possibility of developing a hybrid, blight-resistant species of chestnut, or even some form of inocula-

tion against the blight that would allow for the chestnut's reintroduction from nursery stock.

Members of the environmental establishment frequently
raise the issue of America's disappearing old-growth forests as
evidence of forest decline. The Sierra Club and the Wilderness
Society have been at the forefront in advocating that remaining old-
growth forests be placed in a permanent forest preserve, a position
that was also endorsed by President Bill Clinton during his campaign. Interestingly, the protection of old-growth forests is a
relatively new concern in the environmental movement. Old-growth
forests were once considered the biological deserts of forest ecosystems, as few species are specially adapted to this environment.
Indeed, much of the concern over preserving old-growth forests
seems to arise from an aesthetic preference for forests that have
never been cut, or otherwise disturbed, by humans. Yet there is
little reason to fear the imminent destruction of old-growth forests.
USFS lands still contain over six million acres of old-growth, some
3.3 million of which are protected from timber harvesting.

Deforestation Abroad

Were Theodore Roosevelt and Gifford Pinchot still alive
today, they would be in for a shock. The "timber famine" that they
believed was imminent has been forestalled indefinitely and
America's forests are healthier than at any other time in this century. With continuing technological improvements, the existing trend
of forest growth, led by private owners, should continue.

Unfortunately, the same cannot be said in much of the developing world, where deforestation continues to be the rule rather
than the exception. Government mandates and subsidies from multilateral development organizations like the World Bank have
encouraged rampant deforestation throughout the Third World.
Moreover, poorer nations are often dependent on timber as an energy source, prompting increased levels of cutting, just as was

common in 19th-century America. Whereas America's market economy encouraged a correction of this trend as timber resources became more scarce and prices rose, most developing nations maintain centrally controlled economies under which the reversal of these trends is less likely.

Nonetheless, there are promising signs. Brazil has amended its laws so as to reduce, although not eliminate, the incentive to clear rain forests. Many multinational corporations are now managing forests in a sustainable manner. Yet while the environmental establishment pushes for an international forestry convention negotiated through the United Nations, the best hope for the world's forests lies not in bureaucratic control and multilateral agreements, but rather in the replication of what has worked in the United States: free markets, private property, and technological advance. Then perhaps one day, experts also could speak of the rebirth of forests around the world, not just in America.

Real Rangeland Reform

Robert H. Nelson

For decades, livestock grazing on federal rangelands has been dominated by the outdated progressive-era vision of "scientific management." According to this philosophy, ranchers should not have any firm rights to graze their cattle on public lands. Rather, along with other users, their presence is a "privilege" allowed only so long as government administrators believe it is in "the public interest." Under this approach, federal land agencies are to develop comprehensive plans designed to maximize long-term social welfare from the management of government-owned lands.

In practice, scientific management of public rangelands, like so many dashed hopes of the 20th century, has proven an unworkable utopian vision. Political warfare between ranchers, environmentalists, miners, hunters, and others seeking to press their own claims to the use of the lands is the norm. The resulting "political commons" has had unfortunate consequences all around—including weak incentives to sustain rangeland forage, environmental degradation, and financial losses. Simply put, "scientific management" has failed, and it is time for something different: property rights.

Property rights have been recognized since ancient times as an essential element of a well-ordered society. When clear rights to property exist, the owner will take care to exercise careful stewardship. When rights are undefined, however, there is conflict among multiple claims. In the past, the solution to the confusion of mul-

Excerpted from *How to Reform Grazing Policy* (Washington, DC: Competitive Enterprise Institute, 1996).

Robert H. Nelson

tiple claims on the rangelands in the American West has been government ownership. Ranchers have been allowed to graze livestock on public federal rangelands for over a century. Having applied labor to this land, it stands to reason they are entitled to its benefit. Yet, applying the same thinking, many others have entitlements in the land as well, including conservationists and outdoor enthusiasts.

Many ranchers have pressed for decades for a more formal establishment of their tenure status on the federal rangelands. What is new today is that some prominent members of the environmental movement are beginning to reach a similar conclusion—that a delineation of formal rights-to-use would create an institutional setting that would also promote a more responsible environmental management and use of the federal rangeland resource. The blurred lines of responsibility resulting from the lack of any clear rights on the federal rangelands have been as harmful to the environment as they have been to the conduct of the livestock business.

If "forage access" rights were defined and made legally transferable to any new owner, environmental organizations could purchase the forage rights to federal lands which are now available only to ranchers. Environmental groups seeking to reduce livestock grazing on federal lands would have a realistic way to accomplish their goals without resorting to government regulation. A clear delineation of rights would also encourage existing ranchers to invest in long-run improvement of the land and its productivity. Equally important, the debate over western land-use would no longer be resolved by government planners, but by the competitive workings of the marketplace. Changes in rangeland use would be made through voluntary transactions between existing rights holders—ranchers— and those who wish to see changes on western lands.

Fundamental reform of this sort cannot be accomplished administratively by regulatory agencies. Congress, however, could resolve the long-standing conflict between environmentalists and ranchers by enacting a "Rangeland Homestead Act" to establish a new regime of rangeland rights. Under such a proposal, each holder of an existing grazing permit would be granted equivalent access to rangeland forage as a matter of legal right. Forage access would become a freely transferable property right. As a result, ranchers or other rights holders would have the ability to determine how much and in what manner their rangeland forage would be utilized.

With such new security of tenure, ranchers would have strong incentives to invest with the goal of maintaining the long-term productivity of the land. Private ownership links actions with consequences and thereby promotes responsible management. Insofar as ranchers act as good stewards, the capital value of their forage-access rights would rise as they would be able to sell the rights to any party, whether involved in the livestock business or not.

A new Rangeland Homestead Act would include the abolition of current restrictions that the holder of a grazing permit must be a "qualified" livestock operator and must possess nearby "base property." In addition, the current "use-it-or-lose-it" mandate would be repealed; rights holders would not be required to use their rights for livestock grazing to maintain ownership of them. Unrestricted subleasing would be permitted as well, as is generally the prerogative of the holder of a right.

As noted above, the creation of private rights in the public range would benefit environmental and recreational groups as well. Environmental groups would be allowed to purchase forage-access rights for conservation purposes, such as retiring them to protect riparian habitat. Similarly, hunting clubs could purchase rights to improve wildlife conditions. The Nature Conservancy used this approach to obtain grazing permits on public rangelands in the vicinity of Las Vegas. The grazing rights were not exercised so as to aid the recovery of the desert tortoise, a species listed under the Endangered Species Act. Under current law, however, widespread acquisitions of this kind are difficult and legally uncertain.

Environmental groups have the resources to compete in a market for grazing rights. The total capital value of all grazing permits on Bureau of Land Management lands probably lies between $500 million and $1 billion. Environmental and recreational groups would be interested in only a limited share of all these rangeland forage rights. Thus, they could afford to accomplish their objectives for the range through market purchases. To cut costs, an environmental group could even purchase forage rights and then sublease them to a rancher willing to abide by certain conditions.

Enactment of a Rangeland Homestead Act would give ranchers the security of tenure they have long desired, assuring continued long-run access to forage on public rangelands—at least so long as they chose not to sell. It would provide a channel by which environmental groups could accomplish conservation goals through voluntary transactions with ranchers, rather than through political lobbying and restrictive regulations. Hunters and recreationists would also have equal opportunity to obtain control over the use of forage.

Long term, it might be possible to move beyond government ownership of the Western range altogether. In place of the federal rangelands, there could be a new system of private property rights in which the newly defined rights would include a complex blend of individual and collective rights. An appropriate institutional model here might be a condominium in which the rights to the entire property are separated into the individual rights of the unit owners and the rights to control the use of the common elements that are exercised collectively through the home owners' association or other collective decision-making instrument. In a rangeland condominium, the individually held rights would be the forage rights, giving them control over the use of the grazing forage resource in a particular allotment. In order to implement a full condominium privatization, many more details beyond the brief sketch offered here would have to be provided.

A clearer resolution and formal codification of rancher rights on the federal lands could be a first step toward such broader institutional changes. Under such an approach, rangeland forage would be put to the highest and best use, as revealed in the market by various groups' willingness to pay. As a result, environmental concerns would receive greater consideration on the Western range. In addition, the government would save administrative costs because there would be less need for it to serve as referee or price-setter among constantly warring parties. It would, in short, benefit all parties involved and enhance environmental protection. Much as the creation of property rights solves the tragedy of the commons, creating "forage access" rights could be an important step toward ending the tragic mismanagement of federal rangeland.

Escaping the Malthusian Trap

Gregory Conko and Fred L. Smith, Jr.

On October 12, 1999, United Nations demographers lamented the symbolic birth of planet Earth's six-billionth resident. The world's population had doubled from three billion in less than 50 years. And, though the rate of growth is slowing, population is projected to reach nine billion in another 50 years (Population Division, 1999). Many planners express the traditional Malthusian fears that the earth's ability to feed, clothe, and provide other necessities of life for humanity's growing numbers will soon be surpassed.

While it is indeed wise to recognize the challenge of feeding an additional three billion people, mankind's ingenuity has already provided us an indication of how this can be done. The solution is to ensure that we further liberalize the forces of institutional and technological change that have done so much over the last several centuries to enhance agricultural productivity. Biotechnology is certainly the most promising of these changes. Widespread use of the technologies for recombining plant DNA can help farmers feed the world's growing population, and provide substantial environmental benefits as well.

The fears raised about population growth are not new. Some 200 years ago, the Reverend Thomas Malthus wrote in his *Essay on the Principle of Population* that, if mankind's blind biological urges were left unchecked, population would increase in a geometrical ratio and quickly exhaust the finite resources of nature. "The power of population is indefinitely greater than the power in the earth to produce subsistence for man" (Malthus, 1990). Land could be made

Originally appeared in *AgBioForum*, vol. 2, no. 3 & 4, Summer/Fall 1999.

more productive with more intensive cultivation, but with diminishing marginal returns. Eventual widespread famine was the inevitable fate of mankind.

The Malthusian notion is intuitively appealing. Earth has a finite land mass, and much of it is unsuitable for agriculture or housing. If nothing changes—if we continue to use resources as we do today—then we will indeed "run out" of food. But we need not be content with our current state of knowledge, our current ability to use land to feed ourselves. Indeed, that point eventually came to be realized by Malthus himself. His later work noted that—under the right circumstances and within appropriate institutional structures—impending scarcity could stimulate creative responses to mitigate or curtail resource depletion (Petersen, 1990).

Productivity entails more than simply converting resources into usable products; it means using better ideas—the products of man's ingenuity—to make more with less. "The wellsprings of economic growth are new ideas. People actually improve their lives not through simply using more physical resources, like land, timber, or oil, but by discovering better ways of doing things and novel inventions" (Bailey, 1999). Ideas are invaluable resources because they can be shared, used again and again, and improved upon, all at no additional cost. Most importantly, "humanity cannot deplete the supply of new ideas, designs, and recipes" (Bailey, 1999).

And so it is with agricultural productivity. World farmers did not feed the vastly increased population over the last 50 years by devoting substantially more land or labor to agriculture. Increased food supplies reflect improved crop yields per hectare of arable land. Scientists such as Norman Borlaug and M.S. Swaminathan, along with agronomists from the Consultative Group for International Agricultural Research centers, and a host of other academic and independent scientists, working with government researchers and private corporations, greatly improved the world's knowledge of how to breed better plants and animals, how to produce and better use herbicides, pesticides, and fertilizers. In 1950, world average grain yields were only 1.1 tons per hectare. By 1992, they had risen to 2.8 tons per hectare (FAO, 1992).

But just as some fear the "Gene Revolution," so also did critics of the Green Revolution argue that change was disruptive to traditional societies, that the new technologies were too expensive or environmentally disruptive and hazardous for the peoples of the developing world (Shiva, 1992). Many critics feared that the large-scale use of synthetic pesticides, herbicides, and fertilizers would reduce biodiversity by introducing new toxins into the environment. Others feared that more productive agriculture might encourage the expansion of agriculture into more environmentally sensitive areas, reducing the availability of wildlife habitat.

Of course, the Green Revolution did create some new environmental problems. But it reduced others. The higher yields made possible by the Green Revolution allowed farmers to concentrate production on the best cropland. On balance, Green Revolution technologies promoted environmental values by feeding billions of people *without the need for much additional land*—an important achievement in advancing the overall goal of biodiversity.

By one estimate, improved crop yields from these Green Revolution technologies prevented the conversion of some 3.6 billion hectares of land to agricultural uses since 1961. That would have nearly doubled world cropland from 34 percent of the earth's surface (excluding Antarctica) to 61 percent (Goklany, 1999). "If our technologies had remained stuck in the past and if somehow the world's population had nevertheless been able to grow to its current level, the impact of humanity on the natural environment would have been calamitous" (Bailey, 1999). Technology proved both economically and ecologically valuable.

Yet even during the era of sustained ecological and economic progress, the Neo-Malthusians continuously warned of impending doom. In the very midst of the Green Revolution, Stanford University biologist Paul Ehrlich wrote in his 1968 bestseller, *The Population Bomb*, that "The battle to feed all of humanity is over. In the 1970s the world will undergo famines—hundreds of millions of people are going to starve to death in spite of any crash programs embarked upon now" (Ehrlich, 1968).

The world has experienced severe famines in this century, but they have not been caused by a general lack of food (and have not taken hundreds of millions of lives). Rather, they resulted from political turmoil and non-democratic governments. The work of Nobel Prize-winning economist Amartya Sen demonstrates the importance of liberal democracy, rule of law, and respect for individual rights in ensuring the coordination and delivery of basic economic goods (Sen, 1981). At current levels world food production could provide more than 2,500 calories every day for all six billion people (Goklany, 1999). Ensuring true food security in a world of nine or ten billion, however, will require more than just redistribution.

As if on cue, modern Malthusians have renewed their doomsday message. Yes, we've kept up to date, but *now* (they insist) all possible productivity gains have been exhausted. *Now* disaster lies just around the corner. Consider the recent writing of Worldwatch Institute founder Lester Brown:

> History will likely see the four-decade span from 1950 to 1990 as the golden age in raising world cropland productivity. But the slowdown since then does not come as a surprise, given the inability of scientists to develop a second generation of high-yielding grain varieties that will again double or triple yields. (Brown, et al., 1999)

It will be possible to achieve additional productivity improvements through conventional hybridization. But cross-breeding is a lengthy and imprecise process, and many improvements simply may not be possible with these older techniques. Alternatively, recombinant DNA engineering is much more flexible, precise, and powerful than these earlier methods of genetic manipulation. Because desirable genes coding for specific phenotypical expression from one species can now be more readily identified and integrated into more distant plants and animals, it is very likely that biotechnology could generate the necessary yield increases.

To date, commercially cultivated biotech crop plants have been targeted at farmers in the developed world. The most common ones have been altered to tolerate glyphosate herbicides or to express a *Bacillus thuringiensis* protein, building a pesticide into the plant itself. The future of biotechnology, however, lies in addressing the special problems faced by farmers in the developing world.

Scientists have already identified genes for resistance to common plant diseases and viruses, for drought and cold tolerance (Wambugu, 1999), and for metals and salt tolerance (Moffat, 1999), and, in some cases, have successfully transferred them into crop plants. Once commercially available, farmers in developing countries, where the soils are poor and the climates harsh, are likely to experience dramatic gains in productivity. These improvements are especially important, because as developing nations advance economically, they are unlikely to be satisfied with subsistence-level diets. Though world population is expected to increase by only half, the larger, wealthier population of the year 2050 can be expected to demand more than twice the amount of food produced today (Goklany, 1999).

We should note that the exact rate of productivity improvement is important. If the average annual increase in per-hectare productivity is just 1 percent, the world would have to bring more than 300 million hectares of new land into agricultural use by the year 2050 to meet expected demand; in contrast, a productivity increase of 1.5 percent could double output without the need for additional cropland (Goklany, 1999).

In addition, rDNA techniques offer realistic hope of also improving the nutritional benefits of many foods. Though the bulk of research has focused on increasing crop yields, improving nutritional value is of key importance. Staple crops are good sources of energy, but they are not good sources of micronutrients. The diet of more than three billion people worldwide includes inadequate levels of many important micronutrients such as iron and vitamin A. Deficiency in just these two micronutrients can result in severe anemia, impaired intellectual development, blindness, and even death (DellaPenna, 1999).

Farmers in the developing world often do not have the luxury of growing produce. Fortunately, research into improving nutritional value of staple crops is well underway. Perhaps the most promising recent advance in this area is the development of a rice variety that has been genetically enhanced to increase the level of bioavailable iron and to add beta carotene. The research was funded primarily by the New York-based Rockefeller Foundation, which has promised to make the rice available to developing-world farmers at little or no cost (Rockefeller Foundation, 1999).

Although the complexity of biological systems means that some promised benefits of biotechnology are many years away, the biggest threat that hungry populations currently face are restrictive policies stemming from unwarranted fears that plants genetically enhanced through recombinant DNA technology pose a unique threat to human health or the environment.

This is foolish; rDNA-engineered foods have been among the most closely scrutinized products in memory. They are carefully tested for adverse environmental effects and for possible human allergenicity and toxicity. Biotech crops are planted on more than 70 million acres worldwide, and biotech foods have been consumed in the United States, Australia, and Europe for several years without any recorded adverse effects (Wambugu, 1999). In short, there is no scientifically valid reason to believe that the processes of genetic recombination (as opposed to certain conceivable products) pose any heightened risk.

All change poses some risk. But the minor risks that exist with innovation must be balanced against the massive risks of technological stagnation. The Malthusians have never been right—but the policies they promote could indeed create the disaster they fear. We live in an "Alice In Wonderland" world where we must run to stay in place—we must run much faster to get ahead. For the last few centuries, mankind has indeed run ever faster and has benefited accordingly.

We cannot, of course, be certain that these gains will persist —that mankind's imagination and ingenuity will not flag. But mankind has faced comparable challenges throughout history. Humanity creates problems, but it also solves problems. In the relatively free societies that have led the world in the last few centuries, humanity's ability to imagine and implement technological advances has made it possible to better feed, clothe, and supply energy to ever more people throughout the world. Ensuring that biotechnology remains a viable tool to continue this process is critical. Yet, that requires that the anti-technology policies promoted by our modern Malthusians be defeated.

References

Bailey, Ronald, "The Progress Explosion: Permanently Escaping the Malthusian Trap," in Ronald Bailey, ed., *Earth Report 2000: Revisiting the True State of the Planet* (New York: McGraw-Hill, 1999).

Brown, L.R., et al., *State of the World 1999* (New York: W.W. Norton & Company, 1999).

DellaPenna, D., "Nutritional Genomics: Manipulating Plant Micronutrients to Improve Human Health," *Science*, 285, July 16, 1999, pp. 375-379.

Ehrlich, Paul, *The Population Bomb* (New York: Sierra Club-Ballantine, 1968).

FAO, *FAO Production Yearbook 1992* (Rome: Food and Agriculture Organization, 1992).

Goklany, I.M., "Meeting Global Food Needs: The Environmental Trade-Offs Between Increasing Land Conversion and Land Productivity," *Technology*, vol. 6 (1999), pp. 107-130.

Malthus, T.R., *An Essay on the Principle of Population*, P. James, ed. (London: Cambridge University Press, 1990; original work published 1798).

Moffat, A.S., "Engineering Plants to Cope with Metals," *Science*, 285, July 16, 1999, pp. 369-370.

Petersen, W., "Malthus: The Reactionary Reformer," *The American Scholar*, vol. 59 (Spring 1990), p. 280.

Population Division of the Department of Economic and Social Affairs of the United Nations Secretariat, "The World at Six Billion," Working Paper ESA/ P/WP 154 (New York: Population Division of the Department of Economic and Social Affairs of the United Nations Secretariat, 1999).

Rockefeller Foundation, "New rices may help address vitamin A and iron deficiency, major causes of death in the developing world," press release, August 3, 1999.

Sen, A., *Poverty and Famines: An Essay on Entitlement and Deprivation* (New York: Oxford University Press, 1981).

Shiva, V., *The Violence of the Green Revolution: Third World Agriculture, Ecology and Politics* (London: Zed Books, 1992).

Wambugu, F., "Why Africa needs agricultural biotech," *Nature*, 400, July 1, 1999, pp. 15-16.

Wasting Away

James V. DeLong

Everyone knows that the United States faces a crisis over Municipal Solid Waste (MSW). We are running out of space in which to discard the mountains of trash created by a uniquely wasteful, throw-away, consumerist society. Unless draconian action reduces the volume of trash generated, the situation will become intolerable. Public health will deteriorate as groundwater is poisoned and we will all disappear beneath a revolting melange of plastic wrappers, disposable diapers, rotting offal, old newspapers, and compact disc boxes. A recent poll found that 23 percent of women believe garbage is the most important environmental problem.[1] An Assistant Administrator of the Environmental Protection Agency (EPA) warns us that "at the same time that we generate more waste, we are running out of places to dispose of it," and that this necessitates "a fundamental change in the nation's approach to producing, packaging and disposing of consumer goods."[2] Vice President Al Gore comments on the larger implications: "One of the clearest signs that our relationship to the global environment is in severe crisis is the floodtide of garbage spilling out of our cities and factories."[3]

Everyone also knows the nation is responding: Under pressure, corporations are converting plastic fast-food packaging to degradable materials and reducing packaging volume. Families are returning to cloth diapers. Municipalities are now operating almost 170 waste-to-energy incinerators.[4] Cities are taking funds from low-priority programs (education, police, etc.) to subsidize recycling

Excerpted from *Wasting Away: Mismanaging Municipal Solid Waste* (Washington, DC: Competitive Enterprise Institute, 1994).

programs, and in the past few years the number of municipal curbside collection programs has gone from 600 to over 5,000.[5] European nations are pioneering methods to force manufacturers to retrieve used products and packaging, and US environmentalists and the EPA are pushing to emulate them. States and cities are imposing ordinances controlling product content or packaging, or banning products outright, and states are trying to shut down interstate traffic in wastes.

There are two problems with this depiction of the MSW crisis. The first is that the notion of impending catastrophe is silly. Viewed calmly, with even minimal respect for the data, MSW is a minor national housekeeping problem. The space crisis is as mythical as the unicorn, and other horrors depicted by conventional wisdom are equally ephemeral. MSW represents the type of issue that a competent society should handle routinely, without noticeable stress. All that is required is sensible incentive structures and minor institutional adaptations. Unless MSW disposal is bungled beyond belief, MSW will constitute no threat to the environment or to human health.

The second problem is much more serious. The recital of responses to the "crisis" is true. These efforts, and many more, are indeed occurring, and they are for the most part pointless, wasteful, and both environmentally and economically destructive. At present, the most serious problem facing many local governments is not a glut of garbage but a *shortage*; they have overbuilt processing centers and incinerators, and not enough trash is generated to keep these operating at an economical scale.[6] Packaging practices are not particularly extravagant. Even if they were, the proper response would be a yawn rather than a tirade of righteous indignation, given the trivial impact of packaging on disposal capacity and the substantial mischief that is accompanying attempts to control it. Some genuine problems (and they are *problems*, not crises) might exist, such as hazardous substances tossed into the household trash and some special wastes, such as batteries, but even these are not too serious.

92 ❖ Ecology, Liberty & Property

The dominant impact of the private and public hysteria over MSW is to create a crisis where none existed, and then render it insoluble. The true crisis is that US social and political institutions have become so inept that they cannot deal even with an issue as trivial as this one. The proper approach to MSW is like a case study from an elementary economics text. Governments can establish a few basic rules to keep private-sector actors from dishing costs off onto others or establishing monopolies. Operating within this framework, disposal companies, truckers, railroads, municipal officials, recyclers, waste generators, and others can all perform their respective functions, and the problem will evaporate.

If government cannot arrive at such a policy in an area as simple as MSW, there is cause for utter despair over its capacity to deal with environmental problems of greater complexity and magnitude. The real public concern should be with the symbolic thinking, institutional gridlock, cynicism, rent-seeking, and devotion to hype that have transformed MSW into a "crisis," which are then used as justification for irritating intrusions into the daily life of the citizenry and expensive interference with the operations of whole industries.

Municipal Solid Waste is the waste generated by private households, commercial establishments, and institutions, and picked up by local public or private trash collectors. According to EPA estimates, the nation produced approximately 195 million tons of MSW in 1990.[7] This figure is in line with a general trendline showing an increase of about 5 percent per year. About 55 percent of this waste is generated by households and the rest by commercial establishments and institutions.[8] 195 million tons-per-year of MSW sounds like a lot of garbage. The EPA notes that a year's worth of solid waste loaded into trucks would form a convoy reaching around the world six times or halfway to the moon.[9] Such figures were enough for a popular newsweekly to blazon "Buried Alive" across the cover to promote a feature story on the garbage "crisis" and the imminent exhaustion of landfill space.[10]

The impressiveness of the 195 million-ton statistic dwindles upon reflection. The United States is a big country, and it generates big numbers for everything. If the nation's 260 million people were laid end-to-end they would reach around the world 11 times. The United States has 1.5 billion miles of telephone wire, enough to wrap around the equator 60,316 times. It also consumes 72 billion pounds of fruits and vegetables and produces 68 quadrillion Btus (British Thermal Units) of energy each year.[11]

For these and all other big numbers, the question is, so what? Before succumbing to hysteria one should translate them into practical terms. For MSW, the practical import of 195 million tons is ·small. Compressed to the 30 pounds-per-cubic-foot density prevalent in modern landfills and piled onto a single square mile of land, the pile would be less than 470 feet high. This would be a respectable hill, perhaps a serious tourist attraction, but in a country with almost three million square miles of territory (not counting Alaska), much of which is quite desolate, it would hardly present a problem.

The annual total of 195 million tons of MSW means, on average, each state must find 1.5 million cubic yards of landfill capacity per year. A single abandoned 160-acre farm might do the job nicely for about 30 years. Even crowded, ecologically sensitive New York state has been able to identify 200 square miles of its territory that are suitable for landfills.[12] Clark Wiseman of Gonzaga University determined that all of the solid waste produced in this country over the next one thousand years could fit in a single giant mega-landfill 300 feet deep and less than 30 square miles in area.[13]

One can quibble with these numbers in various ways, adjusting the estimates of waste density or of the basic quantity of MSW, but the conclusion is inescapable: Finding sufficient space for MSW disposal presents no real national problem, and this conclusion is not sensitive to disputes over details.

Were the volume of MSW to become a real concern, considerably greater density can be achieved (at a price, of course) by serious attention to compression. A Japanese company markets an industrial-strength machine that applies 2,800 pounds-per-square-inch of pressure to mixed waste, creating a one-yard cube with a density of over 2,000 pounds-per-cubic-yard, or 74 pounds-per-cubic-foot. This not only reduces space needed for disposal, but the blocks can be covered with concrete and used for construction.[14]

Real environmental problems may exist, but MSW is not among them. The proper approach to the "MSW crisis" is clear: Trash disposal is a commodity, like coal or asparagus, and should be treated accordingly. The role of governments should be minimal. One could argue that governments should not even be in the business of picking up household trash. If property rights are appropriately defined so as to prevent cost-shifting, most communities would realize a vast improvement from complete privatization. It can be argued that cities will have to retain MSW-collection functions because householders who chose not to contract with private haulers could impose excessive costs on neighbors, and policing against midnight dumping would be practically impossible. This issue, combined with the assumption that only governments could attain requisite economies of scale, was what led to the growth of MSW collection in the 19th century. The argument sounds reasonable, but it is not clear that private hauling combined with common law nuisance standards would not provide superior results.

It can also be argued that governments need to be involved to prevent other types of cost-shifting, such as those imposed by inadequate landfill design or lax transportation practices. A landfill owner might choose to allow dumpers to poison the groundwater, taking his fees and moving elsewhere while his former neighbors were left to cope.

These problems would justify regulatory floors of good-management practices for MSW disposal, but they define the outer limits of the appropriate government role in MSW management. Governments should establish reasonable standards to protect the environment from such externalities and costs-shifting, and then do absolutely nothing else. Congress should not permit the states to inhibit free movement of trash, and local ordinances should not extend beyond preventing disposal facilities from shoving costs onto their neighbors. Alternative waste-fee systems should be explored, such as variable rate fees proportional to the weight or volume of trash that is disposed, and cities should vigorously pursue competitive bidding and privatization of services.[15]

Operating within this framework, waste disposal companies, truckers, railroads, municipal officials, recyclers, waste generators, and others could all perform their respective functions. The result would be a complex amalgam of regional landfills, short- and long-haul transportation by truck and rail, waste-to-energy facilities, destructive incineration, market-driven recycling, and source reduction. The mix would vary from place to place depending on the specific characteristics of the city and area. A few thousand acres of land per year, scattered across the 50 states, would be devoted to disposing of MSW. Waste disposers would pay landowners with potential sites for the privilege, and many would be glad to get the money.[16] Recycling would increase as technological hurdles are overcome, but develop in orderly fashion in response to technical advances in market conditions and not by government fiat. In a few years people would wonder what the shouting was about.

At the moment, the chances for such a benign outcome seem dim. Many environmentalists are uninterested in economic and technical arguments, and the general populace has now been subjected to more than 10 years of propaganda about the issue. The idea that there is a crisis is powerful.

If there is to be reform of this issue, it will have to come from a combination of several forces:

- The most important force would be a knowledgeable populace, that understands the sham reasoning underlying present policies.

The growing number of publications questioning the virtue of current policies is a hopeful sign. The failings of the German Green Dot program may also turn out to be a useful tool for the education of the American people.

- Another powerful potential force is the officials of the munici- palities that bear the immediate cost impact. They can pressure their Congressional delegations and state governments to stop acting destructively themselves, and to keep the EPA from act- ing destructively. Success would allow normal economic processes to work.

- Another possible source of rationality is the affected industries. These companies have a problem, of course. Anxious not to ap- pear anti-environment, they have embraced many of the trendy approaches, and by doing so have surrendered to the faulty un- derlying premises about the space crisis, the need for source reduction, and the mystique of recycling. Industry's problem is that the demands escalate as each successive policy proves insuf- ficient, and, having bought off on the existence of a crisis, industry finds it hard to find any stopping place. At some point, enlight- ened self-interest may move industries to begin to refute the premises underlying current policies.

In the end, the MSW problem may be trifling, but the larger stakes are not. The arguments against the current trend of policy are not just economic, they are *moral*. As the Soviets learned, a com- mand-and-control economic system based on some inchoate sense of morality creates a network of industries that actually subtract value. They use resources worth more than the value of the goods pro- duced. The resulting waste lowers the standard-of-living, worsening the lot of the people. MSW policy should be driven by economic and technical realities, not by preconceptions or sentimentality.

James V. DeLong

Notes
1. Anonymous, "Garbage Grows as a Problem, at Least in Some People's Minds," *Wall Street Journal,* March 10, 1994.
2. J. Winston Porter, in "The Solid Waste Dilemma: An Agenda for Action," Final Report of the Municipal Solid Waste Task Force, EPA/530-SW-89-019 (Office of Solid Waste, 1989), at unpaginated and untitled introduction.
3. Al Gore, *Earth In the Balance: Ecology and the Human Spirit* (New York: Houghton Mifflin, 1992), p. 145.
4. Eileen B. Berenyi and Robert N. Gould, "Municipal Waste Combustion in 1993," *Waste Age* (November 1993), p. 51.
5. Christopher Boerner and Kenneth Chilton, "The Folly of Demand Side Recycling," *Environment* (Jan/Feb 1994), pp. 6-8. This is a rough estimate; other sources give different numbers.
6. Jeff Bailey, "Economics of Trash Shift as Cities Learn Dumps Aren't So Full," *Wall Street Journal,* June 2, 1992; John Holusha, "Here's a Switch: Now They're Fighting Over Garbage," *New York Times,* January 23, 1994; Jay Matthews, "Too Much Haste, Not Enough Waste," *Washington Post,* October 30, 1993.
7. *Characterization of Municipal Solid Waste in the United States: 1992 Update,* EPA/530-S-92-019, July 1992.
8. Judd Alexander, *In Defense of Garbage* (New York: Praeger, 1993), p. 18.
9. Quoted in A. Clark Wiseman, "Government and Recycling: Are We Promoting Waste?" *Cato Journal,* vol. 12 (Fall 1992), p. 444.
10. "Buried Alive," *Newsweek,* November 27, 1989, cover.
11. *Statistical Abstract of the United States,* at Tables 17, 902, 928, and 1136.
12. Alexander, *In Defense of Garbage,* p. 155.
13. Wiseman, "Government and Recycling," p. 445.
14. NSWMA, "Putting the Squeeze on Landfills," *Waste Age* (April 1991), p. 58.
15. Some of these options are outlined in Angela Logomasini, "Municipal Solid Waste Mismanagement: Government and Private Alternatives," *Journal of Regulation and Social Costs* (June 1993).
16. Jeff Bailey, "Some Big Waste Firms Pay Some Tiny Towns Little For Dump Sites," *Wall Street Journal,* December 3, 1991; Martha Hamilton, "Environment vs. Jobs: Landfill Proposal Divides West Virginia Town," *Washington Post,* November 4, 1990.

❖❖❖ **Wildlife**

Property Rights in Wildlife

Robert J. Smith

Many conservationists paint a dismal picture of humanity's impact on wildlife. Rapid population growth, more efficient means of capture and kill, and expansion into new continents, some warn, have combined to push more and more species to the brink of extinction. There is no doubt that many animal species are imperiled, and others have become extinct, due to human activity.

The passenger pigeon, which was native to North America, was once probably the most numerous species of bird on earth. At its peak, its population may have numbered around three billion. Its migrating flocks darkened the skies over towns and cities and sounded like an approaching tornado. Yet by 1914, the passenger pigeon was extinct, largely due to over-hunting. A similar fate befell the great auk, a large flightless seabird that nested in vast numbers on islands in the North Atlantic. It was exterminated by whalers and fishermen who slaughtered it for food, eggs, feathers, and oil. Yet just as these and other species declined, populations of other species soared.

Why are some species disappearing and others thriving? It is true that the prairie chicken nearly vanished—the heath hen is extinct, the Atwater's greater prairie chicken has been reduced to endangered species status, and the rest are uncommon, localized, and greatly reduced in numbers—but what about other chickens? Why is the Atwater's greater prairie chicken on the endangered spe-

Originally appeared in *Cato Journal*, vol. 1, no. 2 (Fall 1981), and republished as *Resolving the Tragedy of the Commons by Creating Private Property Rights in Wildlife* (Washington, DC: Center for Private Conservation, 1996).

cies list but not the Rhode Island Red, the Leghorn, or the Barred Rock? These chickens are not even native American birds. They came to this continent with the first European settlers, and the small flocks at the settlement in Jamestown, Virginia, in 1607 became the basis for a broiler industry that produces three billion birds a year.[1]

Similar questions can be asked: Why was the American buffalo nearly exterminated but not the Hereford, the Angus, or the Jersey cow? Why are salmon and trout habitually overfished in the nation's lakes, rivers, and streams, often to the point of endangering the species, while the same species thrive in fish farms and privately owned lakes and ponds? Why do cattle and sheep ranchers over-graze public lands but maintain lush pastures on their own property? Why are rare birds and mammals taken from the wild in a manner that often harms them and depletes the population, but carefully raised and nurtured in aviaries, game ranches, and hunting preserves?

In all of these cases, it is clear that the problem of overexploitation or overharvesting is a result of the resources being under public rather than private ownership. The difference in their management is a direct result of two totally different forms of property rights and ownership: public property and the commons versus private property. Wherever we have public ownership, or an open-access commons, we find overuse, waste, and extinction; but private ownership results in sustained-yield use and preservation.

Commons problems involving wildlife have been especially prevalent in America, and they continue to be extremely vexing precisely because of American wildlife law. The President's Council on Environmental Quality has stressed that "under US law, native wildlife belongs to the people; it is not private property, even on private land."[2] In Europe, however, native wildlife often belongs to private landowners or is managed under a combination of private and public property. Some European countries have fewer problems of overexploitation of wildlife, regardless of population pressures and economic and political systems. In other words, we find precisely what economic analysis has predicted about the treatment of common property and private property wildlife resources.

Lessons from the Fur Trade

An especially illustrative example of private property rights in wildlife appears in the Montagnais Indians of Quebec and Labrador.[3] The Montagnais dwelled in the forests of the Labrador Peninsula, hunting such furbearing animals as caribou, deer, and beaver. They treated wildlife as a public property resource, with everyone sharing the bounty of the hunt. Because game was plentiful and the Indian population was relatively low, the public property resource system worked. "The externality was clearly present. Hunting could be practiced freely and was carried on without assessing its impact on other hunters. But these external effects were of such small significance that it did not pay anyone to take them into account."[4]

However, with the arrival of the French fur traders in the 1600s, the demand for beaver began to rise rapidly. As the value of the furs rose, there was a corresponding increase in the exploitation of the resource. Increasing use of the common property resource would have led to overexploitation of the beaver. With the beaver increasing in value, scarcity, depletion, and localized extinction could be predicted under the existing system of property rights. But unlike the buffalo, virtually condemned to extinction as public property, the beaver were protected by the evolution of private property rights among the hunters. By the early- to mid-18th century, the transition to private hunting grounds was almost complete and the Montagnais were managing the beaver on a sustained-yield basis.[5]

It was a highly sophisticated system. The Montagnais blazed trees with their family crests to delineate their hunting grounds, practiced retaliation against poachers and trespassers, developed a seasonal allotment system, and marked beaver houses. Animal resources were husbanded. Sometimes conservation practices were carried on extensively. Family hunting territories were divided into quarters. Each year the family hunted in a different quarter in rotation, leaving a tract in the center as a sort of bank, not to be hunted over unless forced to do so by a shortage in the regular tract.[6]

This remarkably advanced system lasted for over a century and certainly served to prevent the extinction of the beaver. Unfortunately, more European settlers entered the region and began to treat the beaver as a public property resource, trapping them themselves rather than trading with the Indians, and the beaver began to disappear. Finally, the Indians were forced to abandon their private property system and joined the whites in a rapid overexploitation of the beaver. Baden, Stroup, and Thurman sum up this sorry return to a public property system:

> With the significant intrusion of the white trapper in the 19th century, the Indian's property rights were violated. Because the Indian could not exclude the white trapper from the benefits of conservation both joined in trapping out the beaver. In essence, the Indians lost their ability to enforce property rights and rationally stopped practicing resource conservation.[7]

The Role of Profit

Another example of how private ownership can successfully preserve wildlife is found on game ranches, hunting preserves, safari parks, and animal and bird farms. Many of these private ventures, especially the game ranches, were established to generate profits from private hunting. Consequently, there has been a tremendous outcry from environmentalists and conservationists because the animals are raised for profit and some of them are killed. Yet, if emotional responses can be put aside, it seems clear that these game ranches produce many positive results. Many of the animals they stock are rapidly disappearing in their native countries because of pressures resulting from a rapidly expanding human population. Native habitats are disappearing through the encroachment of agriculture, cattle grazing, timber harvesting, and desertification arising from overexploitation of common property water resources, overgrazing of grasslands, and overutilization of brush, scrub, and trees for firewood and shelter. So serious are these problems and so insoluble under a common property system that there is little hope of saving many species of wildlife in the developing countries. Indeed, some of the more spectacular and most sought-after big-game mammals may now have healthier and more stable populations on some of the game ranches than in their native countries.

Many environmentalists bemoan the fact that the once free-roaming animal herds of the African continent are now kept in captivity for the benefit of American hunters and safari park visitors. But free-roaming is a relative concept. These animals are certainly free-roaming within the boundaries of the game ranches, and many of these ranches are enormous. Furthermore, as the African plains are increasingly delimited with hostile political boundaries and with warring armies and starving populations, there seems little point in mounting campaigns against so-called immoral game ranches and preserves. The growth of agriculture and cattle ranching in these countries is also restricting the free-roaming nature of the wildlife herds.

If the profits gained by giving hunters access to exotic game can provide the economic incentive for these landowners to manage the animals on a sustained-yield basis, some species will be saved. The same holds for the profits to be derived from visitors to game parks and preserves. In fact, the protection provided at some of the parks, preserves, and gardens has actually produced a glut of some animals. There have been well-publicized efforts by some preserves to return their surplus animals to Africa. Lions from America have even been taken to Africa to appear in movies that were filmed there. While we read of zoological parks attempting to discover reversible birth control techniques in order to control their tiger populations, we continue to read about the never-ending difficulties of preserving the remaining tigers in the wild.

Perhaps we should judge all of these activities by their achievements rather than their motives, for it may turn out in the future developing countries will be restocked with their native fauna from specimens now thriving on game ranches and preserves. Already, the books on disappearing wildlife abound with stories of captive breeding of birds and mammals and the successful preservation of species that have either become extremely rare or have disappeared entirely in the wild. Among the many mammals in this category are Père David's deer, which does not exist in the wild and was "discovered" living in the royal zoological park in Peking. It has been saved from extinction by breeding in zoos and private parks. The European bison, or wisent, was reduced to three animals in 1927 and now survives in preserves in Poland. There are similar stories for the Asiatic lion, Prsewalski's Mongolian wild horse, the Arabian oryx, the wild ass or onager, and the Bactrian camel.

Another such success story has been the preservation of the Hawaiian goose, or nene. Once they numbered over 25,000 in the wild, but under common property management the population had plummeted to 20 to 30 birds by 1949. Fortunately, they had been bred by aviculturists as early as 1824. A Hawaiian rancher had many on his farm, and there was a flock at the Wildfowl Trust at Slimbridge, England. Through the combined efforts of many interested parties, an intensive captive breeding program was begun in the United States and Europe, and thousands of young nenes were produced. Beginning in the 1960s, they were reintroduced to the wild in Hawaii, and by the mid 1970s there were as many as 600 in their native habitat.[8]

Private Property over Common Property

In all of these examples it is clear that the single most important element in wildlife survival was their removal from common ownership. Under private property ownership, others were prevented from exploiting the resource, and there were incentives for the owners to preserve them. Furthermore, these incentives were not solely motivated by the possibility of economic gain. With the exception of game ranches, economic gain has seldom been the primary motivation behind most captive breeding projects. Many of these examples were fostered for the pleasure of owning and breeding attractive or rare wildlife, as well as for more "altruistic" reasons, such as a deep commitment to the preservation of vanishing wildlife. Private ownership includes not only hunting preserves, commercial bird breeders, parrot jungles, and safari parks, it also includes wildlife sanctuaries, Audubon Society refuges, World Wildlife Fund preserves, and a multitude of private, non-profit conservation and preservation projects.

The problems of environmental degradation, overexploitation of natural resources, and depletion of wildlife all derive from their existence as common property resources. Wherever we find an approach to the extension of private property rights in these areas, we find superior results. Wherever we have exclusive private ownership, whether it is organized around a profit-seeking or nonprofit undertaking, there are incentives for the private owners to preserve the resource. Self-interest drives the private property owners to careful management and protection of their resource.

It is important not to fall into the trap of believing the different results arising from these two forms of resource management can be changed through education or persuasion. The methods of using or exploiting resources are inherent in the incentives necessarily a part of each system. The overuse of common resources and the preservation of private property resources are both examples of rational behavior by resource users. It is not a case of irrational versus rational behavior. In both cases we are witnessing rational behavior, for resource users are acting in the only manner available to them to obtain any economic or psychological value from the resource.

It has nothing to do with the need for a new environmental ethic. Asking people to revere resources and wildlife won't bring about the peaceable kingdom when the only way a person can survive is to use up the resource before someone else does. Adopting a property system that directs and channels man's innate self-interest into behavior that preserves natural resources and wildlife will cause people to act as if motivated by a new conservationist ethic.

Any resource held in common—whether land, air, the upper atmosphere and outer space, the oceans, lakes, streams, outdoor recreational resources, fisheries, wildlife, or game—can be used simultaneously by more than one individual or group for more than one purpose with many of the multiple uses conflicting. No one has exclusive rights to the resource, nor can anyone prevent others from using it for either the same or any non-compatible use. By its very nature a common resource is owned by everyone and owned by no one. Since everyone uses it there is overuse, waste, and extinction. No one has an incentive to maintain or preserve it. The only way any of the users can capture any value, economic or otherwise, is to exploit the resource as rapidly as possible before someone else does.

But private ownership allows the owner to capture the full capital value of the resource, and self-interest and economic incentive drive the owner to maintain its long-term capital value. The owner of the resource wants to enjoy the benefits of the resource today, tomorrow, and ten years from now, and therefore he will attempt to manage it on a sustained-yield basis.

Conclusion

The problems of overexploitation and extinction of wildlife appear to derive consistently from their being treated as a common resource. Example after example bears this out. It is also predicted by economic analysis of common resources. The only way to avoid the tragedy of the commons in natural resources and wildlife is to create a system of private property rights.

Private property rights have worked successfully in a broad array of cases to preserve wildlife and resolve the tragedy of the commons. Experience and the logical implications of common property resource theory suggest that private property rights are far superior to state or public property rights partly because of the unambiguous exclusivity of private property rights and the difficult problem of preventing too many from using the public domain under a system of state ownership. Furthermore, private property owners have a direct and immediate incentive not to mismanage their own property, while government owners or managers do not have the same incentives, nor are there many incentives that prevent all of the public from overusing the resources held in the public domain.

The proper path toward resolving the vexing issues of wildlife conservation lies in removing wildlife from the commons and creating private property rights. This entails an outright rejection of the concept that wildlife should be viewed as the common heritage of all mankind. It also poses a direct challenge to the basic philosophical beliefs of many environmentalists. But if we are to resolve the tragedy of the commons and preserve our natural resources and wildlife, we must create a new paradigm for the environmental movement: private property rights in natural resources and wildlife.

Notes
    1. Robert E. Cook, Harvey L. Bumgardner, and William E. Shaklee, "How Chicken on Sunday Became an Anyday Treat," in *The 1975 Yearbook of Agriculture: That We May Eat* (Washington, DC: Government Printing Office, 1975), p. 125.
    2. Council on Environmental Quality, *The Sixth Annual Report of the Council on Environmental Quality* (Washington, DC: Government Printing Office, 1975), p. 257.

Robert J. Smith

3. This remarkable development of private property rights in land and especially in wildlife by an aboriginal people was first treated by anthropologists Frank Speck and Eleanor Leacock. More recently it has been subjected to economic analysis by Harold Demsetz, John Baden, Richard Stroup, and Walter Thurman. See Frank G. Speck, "The Basis of American Indian Ownership of Land," *Old Penn Weekly Review*, January 16, 1915; idem, "A Report on Tribal Boundaries and Hunting Areas of the Malechite Indians of New Brunswick," *American Anthropologist*, vol. 48 (1946); Eleanor B. Leacock, "The Montagnais' Hunting Territory and the Fur Trade," *American Anthropologist*, vol. 56, no. 5, pt. 2, memoir no. 78 (October 1954); Harold Demsetz, "Toward a Theory of Property Rights," *American Economic Review*, vol. 57 (1967), pp. 347-359; and John Baden, Richard L. Stroup, and Walter Thurman, "Good Intentions and Self-Interest: Lessons from the American Indian," in *Earth Day Reconsidered*, John Baden, ed. (Washington, DC: The Heritage Foundation, 1980).

4. Demsetz, "Toward a Theory of Property Rights," pp. 351-352.

5. Baden, Stroup, and Thurman, "Good Intentions and Self-Interest," p. 10.

6. Demsetz, "Toward a Theory of Property Rights," p. 353.

7. Baden, Stroup, and Thurman, "Good Intentions and Self Interest," pp. 10-11.

8. See David R. Zimmerman, *To See a Bird in Peril* (New York: Coward, McCann & Geoghegan, 1975), pp. 113-129.

Herd Mentality
Banning Ivory Sales Is No Way to Save the Elephant

Randy T. Simmons and Urs P. Kreuter

On July 18, 1989, Kenyan President Daniel arap Moi set fire to a 12-ton pyre of elephant tusks valued at nearly $3 million. The tusks had been confiscated from poachers and were burned to demonstrate Kenya's dedication to saving the African elephant by ending trade in ivory. Although hunting elephants has been illegal in Kenya for over a decade, the country's elephant population has fallen from 65,000 in 1979 to 19,000 in 1989, a tragedy that Kenyan wildlife experts blame on poaching for the overseas ivory market.

In Harare, Zimbabwe, by contrast, shops openly sell ivory and hides from elephants culled to prevent rapid population growth in the country's game parks. Part of the proceeds of these sales returns to the game parks. Similarly, two dozen peasant villages in Zimbabwe will earn $5 million next year from the sale of elephant-hunting rights on their communal lands to safari operators. The government of Robert Mugabe sees no contradiction between the protection of elephants and the carefully regulated sale of elephant products. On the contrary, Zimbabwe has found that the best way to protect elephants is to give its citizens the opportunity to benefit from their presence. The result: the elephant population has grown from 30,000 to 43,000 over the past 10 years. In neighboring Botswana, where limited hunting is practiced, the elephant population grew from 20,000 to 51,000 in the same period.

Originally appeared in *Policy Review*, Fall 1989. Reprinted with permission.

There are two conflicting approaches to elephant conservation in Africa today. Kenya's ban on hunting and efforts to suppress
the ivory trade are typical of most of Central and East Africa, and
the results have been disastrous. From 1979 to 1989, Central Africa's
elephant population dropped from 497,400 to 274,800, and East
Africa's from 546,650 to 154,720. Elephants in the game parks
were only slightly better protected than those outside. In East
Africa's parks for example, 56 percent of the elephants were killed
or died in the past 10 years. Outside the parks, 78 percent disappeared. Some projections show elephants could be extinct in East
and Central Africa as early as 2005.

The elephant populations of Zimbabwe, Botswana, Namibia,
and South Africa, however, are *increasing*, and now account for 20
percent of the continent's elephants. These Southern African countries all support conservation through utilization, allowing safari
hunting and tourism on private, state, and communal lands, and the
sale of ivory and hides. The sale of hunting rights and elephant
products gives South Africans an economic stake in elephant conservation. It also helps finance strict enforcement of poaching laws.
South Africa's Kruger National Park, for example, earned $2.5 mil-
lion last year, 10 percent of its annual budget, by selling ivory and
hides from 350 elephants culled for ecological reasons to prevent
overpopulation. (Without culling, elephant populations would increase at a rate of 5 percent a year.) Similar ecologically-based
culling programs and sales have been conducted in Zimbabwe for
years and will commence in Botswana next year.

A Total Ban

Unfortunately, Kenya's approach to wildlife conservation is
dominating international efforts to save the African elephant. A
report issued this June by the Ivory Trade Review Group (ITRG),
an international study group funded primarily by Wildlife Conservation International and World Wildlife Fund(US), concluded, "It

is the ivory trade and hunting for ivory, and not habitat loss or human population increase, that is responsible for the decline in [African] elephant numbers."

Upon release of the ITRG report, Kenya, Tanzania, and international conservation groups called for an immediate worldwide ban on the ivory trade. The United States and the European Community responded with a ban on ivory imports. Japan and Hong Kong, the destinations of most raw ivory, instituted some controls as well. In addition, Kenya and Tanzania requested the secretariat of the Convention on International Trade in Endangered Species of Wild Flora and Fauna (CITES) to list the African elephant on Appendix I. An Appendix I listing would ban all trade in elephant products, including hides as well as ivory.

The African elephant currently is listed on Appendix II, which allows some trade, with permits, in ivory and hide. Permits are allocated under a quota system administered by CITES. The quotas are based on the exporting countries' estimates of a sustainable yield.

Boots and Piano Keys

Elephant ivory has been prized for centuries and is now especially valued in the Far East. Ivory is made into piano keys and carved into chess pieces, figures, and the Oriental signature stamps known as "chops." Uncarved tusks like the ones burned by Kenya sold for $2.50 a pound in 1969, jumped to $34 in 1978, and now fetch over $90. Since an average elephant's tusks weigh 22 pounds, the value of each elephant's ivory is $2,000 today. The hide is worth at least as much as the ivory and is made into boots, wallets, and other leather goods.

Even if income from poaching was not available, many rural Africans would have a powerful incentive to kill elephants. Unlike the Asian elephant, which has been domesticated as a beast of burden and is therefore considered a valued treasure in many Indian communities, the African elephant competes for scarce resources, and frequently destroys human property. As Norman Myers put it in 1981 as he was leaving Kenya after working 20 years as a wild-life ecologist for international conservation organizations:

> Wildlife in Africa is being elbowed out of living space by millions of digging hoes—a far greater threat than the poachers' poisoned arrows. When zebras chomp up livestock's grass, when elephants drink dry savannahland water supplies, when buffalo trample maize crops and when lions carry off prize steers, the animals must go—unless they can pay their way.

East and Central African policies do not allow elephants to pay their way, except through tourism. Tourism does generate income, but not for rural Africa's expanding agricultural population. In countries such as Kenya and Tanzania, where over 80 percent of the people live off agriculture, and human populations are rising at 3 to 4 percent a year, few families are willing to endure hunger so an elephant can live to provide a job for an urban-based tourist guide or a photo opportunity for a foreign tourist.

The simple reality is that elephants compete with people for scarce resources, and rural Africans must benefit if conservation is to be successful. The ITRG argument that the decline in elephant numbers is not due to "habitat loss or human population increase" ignores this reality and the incentive it creates for people to engage in poaching or simply kill off local elephants.

Elephants are not even safe from such human pressures in the parks or wildlife reserves. Rural Africans who want land see a local park as a zoo catering to rich foreigners and resent it greatly. The Serengeti Park in Tanzania, for example, is embroiled in a three-way conflict between wildlife managers, subsistence farmers who want land for crops, and the nomadic Masai cattle herders who regard the park as part of their traditional home.

So little is spent on patrolling the game parks in East and Central Africa that the chances of getting caught poaching are minimal. Game guards are ill equipped, woefully underpaid, and sparsely scattered, and park officials have a powerful incentive to supplement their meager government income by aiding poachers.

High-ranking civil servants, members of royal families, and elected officials have participated in the illegal trade as well. During the mid-1970s, for example, it was revealed that Kenya's top wildlife civil servant, John K. Mutinda, was involved in poaching and smuggling. Hunting was subsequently banned to mollify international fund donors. Tanzania banned all trade in tusks in 1987, yet the Member of Parliament for Songea was caught last year with 105 tusks in his official truck.

The policies of East and Central African countries encourage poaching. Rural people have an incentive to eradicate elephants, law enforcement is underfunded and ineffective, and the political will has not been mustered to control corruption among government officials.

Poachers Shot on Sight

The incentives facing would-be poachers are very different in the southern countries. In Zimbabwe, poachers are shot on sight and over $600 per square mile is spent to protect the wildlife estate. Elephants are marketed extensively under concession permits on state-owned safari areas and communal lands, and managed intensively in the national parks. Hunting and photographic opportunities are sold primarily to an international clientele. The price of an average hunt in Zimbabwe, where elephant is the main trophy, is currently $25,000. With such value at stake, the incentive to protect resident elephants is equivalent to that of protecting domestic livestock.

Ten thousand elephants live on Zimbabwe's communal lands—lands for peasant farmers but without individual ownership of land or wildlife. Rather than rely on prohibitions to protect the elephants, the Zimbabwe Department of National Parks and Wild-life Management gives peasant communities the right to hunt a certain number of elephants. The communities can exercise this right themselves or sell the hunting permits to commercial opera-tors. This has resulted in a much more positive attitude toward wildlife among Zimbabwean villagers.

One Zimbabwean subsistence community recently curtailed poaching in Gona-re-Zhou National Park and villagers withdrew from some land for wildlife in exchange for hunting permits for elephants and buffalo that overflowed from the park. The permits were sold to a safari operator and part of the proceeds were used to develop community facilities, while the rest was distributed directly to community members who lost crops to animal damage.

In addition to hunting permits, further income is generated for rural communities when animals that destroy property are elimi-nated by National Parks personnel. The ivory and hide from these animals belong to the community members. Since at least as many destructive animals as trophy bulls are killed each year, the sales of hides and ivory from marauding elephants represents a substantial component of the income to communal members.

Biological Imperialism

The expansion of Southern African elephant herds suggests that proponents of a global ban on ivory trade are asking the wrong question. They ask, "How do we stop the ivory trade in order to remove the incentive for poaching?" They should ask, "How do we make elephants valuable enough that people have an incentive to be careful stewards rather than careless exterminators?"

And why do they ask the wrong question? Perhaps those who wish to save the elephant are simply misled by the no-trade ideology of many American and European environmentalists—a biological imperialism imposed regardless of local realities and val-ues for wildlife. The second possibility is less benign than good intentions gone astray. It is that an international ban is expected to substituted for effective law enforcement at the national level and to cover up or ignore decades of mismanagement and corruption.

Economic theory teaches that a government ban on the supply of a valued commodity can never wholly eliminate demand. It does accomplish three things, however: prices increase, people with a comparative advantage at avoiding detection—usually criminals and corrupt public officials—take over the formerly legal market, and in the case of resources owned in common, the resource disappears. Legalizing trade and protecting property rights, however, reverses these outcomes: prices drop as the legal supply grows, there is no premium on criminality and corruption, and property rights encourage wise stewardship of the resource.

Parrots in Hubcaps

Trade bans on wildlife products have failed to protect species for which there is a commercial demand. Many species of Latin American parrots, for instance, are "protected" by CITES Appendix I listing. Prices skyrocketed after the trade ban and the legal trade was taken over by poachers who make no effort to maintain birds on a sustainable basis. After all, the nest left today will in all likelihood be taken by someone else tomorrow. Native hunters go so far as to chop down nesting trees to get the parrots. The captured parrots are drugged, put in door panels, and even hubcaps, and smuggled into the United States, where the few that actually survive are sold on the black market for more than $20,000. The return for trading in protected birds is often greater than what can be made from producing illegal drugs. Rather than reducing the slide in native parrot populations, prohibition has accelerated it.

Prohibition has also failed to protect the black rhino. About 50,000 existed in Africa when the 1976 CITES ban went into effect. The rhinos dwindled to 14,000 by 1980, 8,800 by 1984, and only about 3,500 exist today—most of which are in Zimbabwe and South

Africa. Rhino horn is prized by Arabs for dagger handles and by Asians for its supposed value as a medicine and aphrodisiac. It currently sells for about $8,000 per pound and each horn weighs about 10 pounds, making a rhino worth about $80,000. Given such enormous economic values, Zimbabwean officials are moving some black rhinos from the Zambezi Valley, where they are poached by Zambians, to privately owned ranches. Black and white rhino populations have dramatically increased in South Africa.

All wild cats were listed on CITES Appendix I in 1976, and the fact that some leopard populations have been downlisted to allow sport hunting and some export for non-commercial, personal use is sometimes claimed as an Appendix I success. But scientific data did not support listing these populations on Appendix I in the first place and the listing discouraged their preservation. The leopards in Zimbabwe, for example, were not endangered and they posed a serious threat to livestock. Consequently, until the CITES downlisting was approved, leopards were killed in rural areas, not for skin sale, but for predator control.

Even if the probable outcomes of an Appendix I listing are ignored, a further problem remains: reestablishing a legal market once it is destroyed by a trade ban. In the case of American alligators, reestablishing the market in skins has been difficult even as alligator populations have rebounded under commercial management.

Conservation Through Commercialization

Contrary to the poor record of trade bans, commercialization has successfully protected a broad variety of species. Seabirds are farmed in Iceland. Crocodiles and butterflies are raised in Papua, New Guinea. Crocodile farming is a multimillion dollar business in Zimbabwe, and is growing in Malawi. The crocodile has an Appendix I listing in most countries, but Zimbabwe has declared a reservation.

The white rhino, also listed on Appendix I, declined from 1,500 animals spread among five countries in 1960 to just 20 animals in 1989. In contrast, the white rhino population increased tenfold in South Africa during the same period and now totals about 6,000 in parks, reserves, and on privately owned ranches. White rhinos are hunted in South Africa, and the horns from hunting trophies are not presently traded, but would be worth millions of dollars annually that could be spent on additional rhino protection.

Ivory Branding

An international ban on trade in ivory will increase the price of ivory significantly as the black market tries to satisfy consumer demand. Some countries have already established ivory stockpiles in anticipation of such a price rise. The *Economist* reports that Burundi has stashed 90-100 tons and Hong Kong has 500-700 tons set aside. One effect of the price rise will be to encourage more people to become involved in poaching. Likely candidates include the Southern Somali "Shiftas" who roam and plunder at will in northeastern Kenya. A second effect will be to encourage greater political corruption as the returns from aiding illegal shipments will rise with the price of ivory.

In addition, revenue derived from ecologically necessary culling programs in South Africa will be lost, leaving fewer financial resources to protect wildlife from poachers or for controlling expanding elephant herds. Wildlife officials in Zimbabwe believe a ban will make the elephant extinct in communal lands.

Consequently, Zimbabwe, South Africa, Botswana, Malawi, Mozambique, and Zambia have decided not to participate in a ban, and instead are developing a cooperative ivory marketing and control system. This system will include stringent controls and checks to reduce the chances of illegal ivory from other African countries being sold through the system. It will introduce a form of ivory identification, a type of branding, based on chemical analysis, Xray spectrophotometry, electron microscopy, and other forensic techniques. This identification technology can pinpoint the origin of the ivory. Only ivory originating in the countries that join the regional marketing system will be allowed to be sold.

Abrogation of Responsibility

Elephants are endangered in certain parts of Africa, not all Africa. Thus, the solution to saving the African elephant lies not in banning ivory trade, but in applying the successful elephant conservation policies of South African nations to East African nations that have mismanaged their resources. Where poaching and facilitation of poaching by corrupt officials occurs, the responsibility lies with the country's government. An international ban on trade in ivory will not solve internal problems and is an abrogation of responsibility to eliminate the true causes of elephant decline.

If the East and Central African nations sincerely wish to save their elephants they must begin by managing wildlife for the benefit of the human inhabitants of their countries. Current conflicts between people and protected areas must be replaced with a custodial and participatory relationship. To do that, rural Africans must be able to make discretionary use of wildlife.

Bans on hunting need to be replaced with policies that encourage game ranching, safari hunting, and indigenous use of wildlife. And patrolling efforts need to be funded at levels that make poaching too risky.

Zambia, the only Southern African country with a declining elephant population, is adopting just such a strategy in response to losing 75,000 elephants in the Luangwa Valley to poachers this decade despite a ban on hunting. In a policy reversal, they have started trophy hunting and ivory sales, with the proceeds going to pay for increased policing and to benefit local residents.

Commercialization and intensive management of wildlife are difficult concepts for many members of the American wildlife lobby to accept. But there is still time to reconsider. With elephant herds expanding in Southern Africa there is no need for those in East and Central Africa to be rushing toward extinction.

To Save an Endangered Species, Own One

Ike C. Sugg

Ever since 1989, when the Convention on International Trade in Endangered Species banned trade in African elephant ivory, a battle has raged in conservation circles over the property status of wildlife and the role of economic incentives in conserving endangered species. The latest skirmish is being fought over game ranching, perhaps the most promising approach to wildlife conservation yet.

Game ranching is a truly private enterprise. It is the private ownership of wildlife carried out on private property, typically for profit. In the United States, the ownership of domestic wildlife is divided between state and federal governments. Most game ranchers raise "exotics," that is, non-native animals not traditionally farmed or ranched. Those species can be privately owned under US law, whereas their domestic counterparts, with few exceptions, cannot.

Such private ownership has produced some remarkable results. The scimitar-horned oryx, for example, owes its continued existence to the incentives of game ranching. David Bamberger, the former chairman of Church's Fried Chicken and now a game rancher, has single-handedly preserved 29 of 31 remaining bloodlines of this rare antelope, which is virtually extinct in its native sub-Saharan range. Indeed, there are more of these animals on game ranches in Texas than in its war-torn North African home.

Mr. Bamberger is a member of the Exotic Wildlife Association, an international game-ranching organization headquartered in the Texas hill country. He and the 450-plus other members own an estimated 200,000 head of some 125 species. Over 19,000 of those animals belong to species that are threatened or endangered in the wild. Like the oryx, several of them are more plentiful in Texas than in their native ranges. The blackbuck antelope, for example, is ubiquitous on Texas' Edwards Plateau, but only a few still exist in its native India.

Despite the conservation successes of game ranching, however, it is under assault. Effectively outlawed now in several states, with prohibitions pending in others, game ranching is the bane of certain environmentalists, who seem intent on stifling this promising infant industry.

Indeed, Washington state recently closed its borders to non-native wildlife and banned the private owners of non-native species from breeding their animals. California has revoked all import and export permits for non-native hoofstock and is considering a bill to specifically outlaw the game-ranching industry. On the national front, Michael Bean of the Environmental Defense Fund, a leading proponent of the Endangered Species Act, has recommended to a Senate committee that the act be revised to inhibit the private, for-profit propagation of listed species.

The notion of privatizing wildlife is blasphemy in the religion that has become wildlife preservation. One of the major tenets of that religion is that markets decimate species, pushing them toward extinction. In the latest issue of *International Wildlife*, the flagship publication of the National Wildlife Federation, Valerius Geist, one of game ranching's most vociferous opponents, states emphatically, "I won't be satisfied until every last game ranch is shut down.…When man puts a price tag on a wild animal, that wild animal eventually disappears."

But as we have seen with the oryx and blackbuck, quite the opposite is the case. True believers point to the extirpation of the passenger pigeon by hunters at the turn of this century, but here again they misread the evidence. As free-market environmentalist R.J. Smith has pointed out, there were three billion passenger pigeons in America when Europeans arrived, and no chickens. Today there are no passenger pigeons, yet millions of chickens are harvested each year. A price tag was put on both species, as humans once enjoyed eating both. The crucial difference was that chickens were allowed to remain in private hands, where they were bred, while the pigeons belonged "to all citizens in common." Thus, there was no incentive to protect them.

Private ownership is a necessary condition for the species conservation game ranching encourages, but it is seldom sufficient. The success of game ranching depends on markets for its products— whether they are sold for meat, breeding stock or hunting opportunities. Few ranchers, no matter how conservation-minded, would go to the expense and effort of raising wildlife if they could not earn a return off doing so. Thus, the price tag does matter.

So does regulation. When a species is listed as endangered by national or international agencies, it becomes very difficult to buy, sell, propagate, or otherwise handle because of highly restrictive regulations. The incentive to raise listed animals is thus weakened.

After the barasingha (a deer indigenous to India) was listed, many game ranchers quit buying and raising them. This distinctive effect was evident more recently when Mr. Bamberger tried, and failed, to convince other game ranchers to invest in a survival plan for the scimitar-horned oryx. The reason for their reluctance? The Fish and Wildlife Service proposed to list the oryx, along with two other species of African antelopes now raised on game ranches, as "endangered" under the Endangered Species Act.

As Mr. Bamberger laments, "altruism will not save a species." If game ranchers lose interest in a species, its future is imperiled. Those with an economic stake in a natural resource have every reason to conserve and care for it. With wildlife, the pursuit of profit motivates the rancher to maximize that which is valuable, which means increasing wildlife numbers. It means preserving the genetic purity of the species, from which its value is often derived. And it means taking care of the land—a collateral ecological benefit.

Unfortunately, the environmental logic of game ranching, and its successes, will not be enough to save it from the wrath of the high priests of preservationism, for whom the commercial utilization of wildlife is heretical. Their antipathy to markets reinforces one's suspicion that certain preservationists are more anti-capitalists than they are pro-environment.

It should be pointed out that free-market environmentalism does threaten the survival of one protected species in this country, the sacred cow, and is encroaching upon its native habitat inside the Beltway. The admirable achievements of David Bamberger and other game ranchers suggest that this may not be a bad thing.

Fishing for Solutions

Michael De Alessi

The collapse of the once-rich fisheries off the coast of New England is dramatic testimony to the failure of fishery management in the United States. This tragedy has been the result of traditional fishing limits on seasons and gear that ignore the alternatives that people face and that encourage fishermen to vacuum the seas. Fishermen have no desire to destroy their own source of livelihood, but as long as the rules of the game reward overharvesting, fish stocks will continue to decline. As a result, the cod stocks that were once the staple of New England diets are now effectively commercially extinct.

Like the New England fisheries, marine resources around the world have suffered immeasurably from being managed as public resources. Without some sort of private ownership, there has been a corresponding lack of stewardship. Although many of the world's fisheries are in a sorry state, there has been a growing appreciation for *why* some fisheries suffer while others do not, and so attempts to create positive marine stewardship incentives are growing around the world, most notably in Iceland and New Zealand.

Some recent innovations, particularly the Individual Transferable Quota (ITQ), are now working toward changing the motivations of fishermen, not just their harvesting ability. ITQs grant fishermen a right to a percentage of a total harvest, so that healthier fish populations translate into rights to catch a greater number of fish. Because ITQs are also transferable, fishermen can

Excerpted from "Fishing for Solutions," *IEA Studies on the Environment*, no. 11 (London: Institute of Economic Affairs, 1998). Reprinted with permission.

realize the gains from any improvements in the fishery, which encourages them to invest time, effort, and money into research and stewardship. ITQs will not be well-suited to every fishery, and they certainly do not translate into private ownership of actual fish and marine habitat (which would create even stronger stewardship incentives), but they are a definite step in the right direction.

Property Rights, Economics, and Marine Resources

> *"A primary function of property rights is that of guiding incentives to achieve a greater internalization of externalities."*
> —Harold Demsetz (1967, p. 348)

When the ocean's resources are free for the taking, the only way to benefit from them is by extraction. This does not cause problems when fish are plentiful and catches are small, but as the pressure on a fishery grows, so does the potential for depletion. Fishers realize that what they leave behind may simply be caught by someone else, and without any way to benefit from leaving fish in the water, they try to harvest as much as possible. This reduces fish populations and harms the fishery but, since the harmful effects of each fisher's actions are shared by all the participants, they are largely ignored. Catching so many fish that the resource becomes depleted and the livelihood of the fishers destroyed may not make sense when looked at in aggregate, but on an individual level it makes perfect sense. In such a system of open access to a valuable resource with low harvesting costs, there are no rewards for restraint and the rational option for each individual is to fish at an unsustainable rate.

Property rights encourage the internalization of the harms and benefits caused by a particular user or group of users because they determine whether the future effects of current behavior (either positive or negative) will be borne by the owner. Thus, as property rights become more well defined, resource stewardship becomes more attractive and owners bear more of the costs of rapacious behaviour.

The crucial determinant for the private ownership of a resource is that the welfare of the decision-makers is tied to the economic consequences of their decisions (De Alessi, 1980). Individually-parcelled private property rights offer the greatest rewards for conservation to their owners, but are also the most costly to define and enforce. While property rights in oceans may seem particularly difficult to implement, many cultures have recognized such rights for centuries. As John Cordell notes,

> It is one thing to contemplate the inshore sea from land's end as a stranger, to observe an apparently empty, featureless, open accessed expanse of water. The image in a fisherman's mind is something very different. Seascapes are blanketed with history and imbued with names, myths, and legends, and elaborate territories that sometimes become exclusive provinces partitioned with traditional rights and owners much like property on land. (1989, p. 1)

Common Property Rights

The most common form of property rights in marine resources are common property rights, in which the rights are owned by groups, as opposed to individuals:

> Common property régimes are a way of privatizing the rights to something without dividing it into pieces. Historically, common property régimes have evolved in places where the demand on a resource is too great to tolerate open access, so property rights in resources have to be created, but some other factor makes it

impossible or undesirable to parcel the resource itself. (McKean and Ostrom, 1995, p. 6)

Common property rights, like pure private property rights, can help avoid the tragedy that results from the open-access commons.

Common property régimes occur frequently in developing nations, where the relative value of fish tends to be higher, leading to greater competition for their capture and making monitoring and enforcement difficult. Parcelling resources into individual units under such circumstances is often not practicable, whereas vesting group control over a resource may be.

One valuable species that lends itself to common property control is the lobster. In some of these cases, common property régimes arise where private ownership is not a legal option. In the Maine lobster fishery, "harbor gangs" have formed that mark territories and turn away outsiders—an extra-legal common property arrangement (Acheson, 1987). As a result, lobstermen in these gangs have higher catches, larger lobsters, and larger incomes than those who fish outside controlled areas (Acheson, 1987). These gangs are often composed of members of a particular family or individuals of long-standing community membership—exemplifying the importance of homogeneity to successful common property régimes.

Private Property Rights

Clearly defined and readily enforceable private property rights to marine resources are rare. However, those few examples that do exist strongly support the arguments of theorists who have promoted private property rights in the oceans as a means to improve resource management (see, for example, Keen, 1983; Scott, 1988; Jeffreys, 1996; and Edwards, 1994).

One of the few empirical studies of the effects of private property rights on marine resources was done in the 1970s by Richard Agnello and Lawrence Donnelley (1975), economists at the

University of Delaware. They looked at oyster beds in the Chesapeake Bay (in Maryland and Virginia) and in some of the states on the Gulf of Mexico. They compared those managed by state regulators to those owned by private leaseholders and found the leased oyster beds were healthier, better maintained, and produced better quality oysters.

How and why private property rights develop depends on the value of resources and the costs of monitoring them. An early example of the development of private ownership rights can be found in the American West. At the end of the 19th century, land in the American West seemed boundless and plentiful. Much like the oceans not so long ago, one could hardly imagine depleting its vast resources. But as the West was settled, its water and grassy lands became progressively more scarce and more valuable. Research by economists Terry Anderson and P.J. Hill (1975) has shown that, as the rights to these resources became more valuable, more effort went into enforcing private property rights, and therefore into innovation and resource conservation.

Defining private property by physical barriers was desirable, but initially in the West there were too few raw materials for this to be possible, so livestock intermingled and monitoring was difficult. However, frontier entrepreneurs soon developed branding systems to identify individual animals, and organisations such as cattlemen's associations were formed to standardise and register these brands. These branding technologies allowed cattlemen to define and enforce private property rights over a valuable roaming resource.

Then in the 1870s another innovation came along that radically altered the frontier landscape—barbed wire. Barbed wire was an inexpensive and effective means of marking territory, excluding interlopers, and keeping in livestock. It became easier to enclose property and exert private ownership. Innovations such as barbed wire that developed during the westward expansion of the 1800s illustrate how private property rights encourage innovation.

Similar challenges to those faced by the early settlers in the American West are faced today in the oceans. It is often difficult to envision alternative methods of managing natural resources, especially in the marine environment, but wherever private property rights may be asserted, incentives exist to develop methods of fencing and branding no matter what the physical environment. Regrettably, such approaches have rarely been tried.

Government Regulation of Fisheries

Government regulation of fisheries is pervasive world-wide. The results have generally been less than laudable. Waste of resources, time, effort, and capital have not only been encouraged through regulation, but have also frequently been subsidised. The most common forms of government regulation to date ignore the problem of open access and instead attempt to limit fishing harvests with restrictions on fishing gear, effort, and seasons. This adversarial relationship between the regulators and the fishers does little to discourage fishers from harvesting as many fish as possible—fishers are quite adept at staying one step ahead of the latest limitations imposed on them.

In order to circumvent regulations, fishers frequently make large investments in capital—buying bigger boats or larger nets, for example. Indeed, when Frederick Bell (1972, p. 156) studied the northern lobster fisheries in the United States in the 1970s, he estimated that "over 50 per cent of the capital and labour employed in lobstering represent an uneconomic use of factors." Attempts to avoid regulatory restrictions sometimes reach a comical extent. Restrictions on the length of boats lead to very wide boats; limits on the number of nets lead to bigger nets; short seasons lead to very fast boats or boats with more storage and freezer facilities on board. All inevitably lead to complaints that fisheries are overcapitalised.

The Alaskan halibut fishery was an extreme example of regulatory failure. As pressure on this fishery increased, regulators responded by shortening the seasons during which the fish could be caught. The fishing fleet responded predictably by finding ways to catch fish more quickly and before long the entire year's season had been shortened to just two days. The same amount of fish were caught as before, only now the fishery was a dangerous derby, held often in bad weather and with frequent loss of life. Not only that, but fresh fish were only available for a very short time, the fish were handled poorly in the rush, and most fish went straight into the freezer, decreasing their value.

Getting the Institutions Right

The failure of regulation is leading to a search for alternatives. Many countries are beginning to experiment with private approaches to fisheries management. The most common tool to date for this is the Individual Transferable Quota (ITQ), which grants the owner the right to harvest a certain amount of fish in a given year, and can be bought or sold. ITQs have been introduced in recent years in New Zealand, Iceland, Australia, the United States, and Canada.

ITQs are not real private property rights, but they are often a step in the right direction. In contrast to regulation-based government controls, they are incentive-compatible, vesting those who harvest the resource with some incentive to conserve the fishery. They also offer a real opportunity to begin to move towards the private ownership of marine resources.

In many of the places where ITQs have been introduced they have begun to provide neat solutions to complex conflicts, such as native claims to fisheries. ITQs have also reduced the costs of fisheries management by reducing subsidies and reducing fishing capacity. In Alaska, IFQs (Individual Fishing Quotas, a form of ITQs) have eliminated the infamous and dangerous race for fish known as the halibut derby. The fishery there is now less dangerous, there are fewer boats, and fresh, quality halibut is available for many more than two weeks a year.

ITQs are not a panacea, but they are an important recognition of the power of positive incentives for stewardship and conservation. After ITQs were implemented in New Zealand, Philip Major of the Ministry of Agriculture noted, "It's the first group of fishers I've ever encountered who turned down the chance to take more fish" (quoted in *The Economist*, 1994, p. 24). Every fishery is different, and so are the people involved in determining its future. What is acceptable to them is what matters most, and in many cases ITQs may not be considered ideal. Moving in the direction of a private arrangement, however, is crucial to the health of the resource. Even though ITQs rarely approximate private arrangements, they may often be the most feasible step that can be taken in that direction. For that reason alone, they merit serious consideration.

Conclusions

The crash of so many once-plentiful marine fisheries is a clear indication of institutional failure. But there is hope for the future. Evidence indicates that fish stocks are highly resilient and are likely to recover rapidly if given the chance (Myers, et al., 1995). To give them that chance, government should consider turning over the management of fisheries to private interests. Private property, owned individually or in common, offers the best hope of creating incentives for conservation, stimulating the production of new technologies, and protecting the marine environment. Although they may stumble occasionally, mistakes by one individual or group will be more than offset by the successes of others. In the end, the environment, the health of the fish stocks, their harvesters, and the fish-eating public will be better off.

Although traditional environmental groups in both the United States and Europe have generally resisted supporting market measures to improve fisheries management, that is beginning to change. In the United States the Environmental Defense Fund recently strongly supported the creation of ITQs to "give value to fish in the water [and] create positive economic incentives to conserve fish" (Fujita and Hopkins, 1995). From satellite technology used to monitor the oceans to artificial reefs that attract and nurture fish populations to fish farming, technologies exist that could facilitate private ownership in the oceans.

The growing interest in addressing what motivates stewardship is a very positive development, and none too late. Conflicts over ocean space are increasing rapidly as recreational and commercial fishers, oil companies, SCUBA divers, environmentalists, and others all vie for their piece of the pie. To reconcile all of these competing interests, and to prevent further degradation of the marine environment, private ownership, in any of its many forms, is essential.

References

Acheson, J.M., "The Lobster Fiefs Revisited," in McCay and Acheson, eds., *The Question of the Commons* (Tucson: University of Arizona Press, 1987), pp. 37-65.

Agnello, R.R, and L. Donnelley, "Property Rights and Efficiency in the Oyster Industry," *Journal of Law and Economics*, vol. 18 (1975), pp. 521-533.

Anderson, T.L., and P.J. Hill, "The Evolution of Property Rights: A Study of the American West," *Journal of Law and Economics*, vol. 12 (1975), pp. 163-179.

Bell, F.W., "Technological Externalities and Common-Property Resources: An Empirical Study of the U.S. Northern Lobster Fishery," *Journal of Political Economy*, vol. 80 (1972), pp. 148-158.

Cordell, J., *A Sea of Small Boats* (Cambridge, Massachusetts: Cultural Survival, Inc., 1989).

De Alessi, L., "The Economics of Property Rights: A Review of the Evidence," *Research in Law and Economics*, vol. 2 (1980), pp. 1-47.

Demsetz, H., "Toward a Theory of Property Rights," *American Economic Review,* vol. 57 (1967), pp. 347-359.

The Economist, "The Tragedy of the Oceans," March 19, 1994, pp. 21-24.

Edwards, S.F., "Ownership of Renewable Ocean Resources," *Marine Resource Economics,* vol. 9 (1994), pp. 253-273.

Fujita, R., and D. Hopkins, "Market theory can help solve overfishing," *The Oregonian,* September 20, 1995.

Jeffreys, K., "Rescuing the Oceans," in R. Bailey, ed., *The True State of the Planet* (New York: The Free Press, 1996), pp. 295-338.

Keen, E., "Common Property in Fisheries: Is Sole Ownership an Option?" *Marine Policy,* vol. 7 (1983), pp. 197-211.

McKean, M., and E. Ostrom, "Common Property Régimes in the Forest: Just a Relic from the Past?" *Unasylva,* vol. 46, no. 180 (1995), pp. 3-15.

Myers, R.A., et al., "Population Dynamics of Exploited Fish Stocks at Low Population Levels," *Science,* 269 (1995), pp. 1106-1108.

Scott, A., "Development of Property in the Fishery," *Marine Resource Economics,* vol. 5 (1988), pp. 289-311.

 **Pollution Control**

Making the Polluter Pay

Jonathan H. Adler

Environmentalists often call for a world with zero pollution. The response from industry and professional economists is disbelief. Who is right? That depends upon how one defines pollution. Assuming that pollution is properly defined, government *should* seek to reduce pollution as much as is possible—perhaps even to eliminate it altogether. However, if pollution is improperly defined, "pollution control" can become a pretext for the federal government to regulate the minutiae of each and every industrial process and economic transaction.

Emissions *per se* are not pollution. Pollution is the imposition of a harmful waste product or emission onto the person or property of another without that person's consent; it is a "trespass" under the principles of common law. If the trespass is so minor that it creates no impact or inconvenience for the property owner, it will normally be tolerated. Otherwise, it will likely result in legal action of some kind. Today's pollution dilemma is often the result of what is essentially a universal "easement" granted by the state to polluters, even to producers of significant and damaging pollution.

Because the first duty of government should always be to protect people and their properties from external harm, pollution control is a legitimate function of government.[1] Pollution, like vandalism or theft, deprives people of what is theirs. The proper role for government in this area is to ensure that polluters pay for the damage they cause and are enjoined from causing harm in the future. This approach is often referred to as the "polluter pays

Adapted from an essay originally published in *The Freeman*, March 1995.

principle," and was trumpeted by early environmentalists as a means to discourage environmental harms such as those that caused the Cuyahoga river to catch fire. If companies paid a price for polluting, it was argued, they would be less likely to do it.[2]

However, this approach is rarely embodied in American environmental laws. The rhetoric of "polluter pays" is often used, but rarely in connection to forcing particular polluters to pay for actual damage. In the case of Superfund, for example, "polluter pays" was used to justify generic taxes on particular industries, irrespective of the relative contributions of specific corporations to actual environmental damage.

Current environmental policy too rarely focuses on harm and too often focuses on compliance with Byzantine rules and requirements. Fines are levied not when the property of another is contaminated, but when a permit is improperly filed, or a waste-transport manifest is not completed in line with the demands of regulatory officials. As the Environmental Protection Agency has observed, "a regulated hazardous waste handler must do hundreds of things correctly to fully comply with the regulations, yet doing only one thing wrong makes the handler a violator."[3]

Environmental rules are now so complex that only 30 percent of corporate counsels believe that full compliance with environmental laws is actually possible, according to a survey conducted by the *National Law Journal*.[4] This is astonishing evidence that many pollution-control efforts are misdirected. The proper focus of government officials should be identifying and prosecuting those firms that tangibly threaten human health and environmental properties, instead of monitoring compliance with overly-complex and time-consuming permitting and paperwork requirements.

We are all familiar with the case of the Exxon *Valdez*. An oil tanker ran aground because of an allegedly drunken captain, and over 300,000 barrels of crude oil poured into the water of Prince William Sound, causing significant (though not permanent) environmental disruption. What few are aware of, however, is the crime for which Exxon was punished was killing migratory birds without a permit. Extensive shorelines were covered in oil, and the government prosecuted Exxon for not having permission to go hunting!

Exxon was subject to civil suits from those, such as local fishermen, that claimed damage from the spill. However, much of the money that Exxon was forced to pay did not go to alleged victims of the spill. Exxon was required to pay $125 million in fines to the federal government and the state of Alaska. In addition, Exxon was forced to pay $900 million into a fund to be doled out by government officials for environmental projects, habitat protection, and scientific research, among other things.[5] Last May, $38.7 million of this money was used to create a new state park.[6]

Even the money spent on cleanup was misspent. Exxon was under tremendous political pressure to restore the "public" shoreline. Thus it engaged in an extensive and costly cleanup operation. However, not only was much of the cleanup unnecessary—nature has its own methods of cleaning up spills of natural substances like oil—but in some cases the extensive beach cleaning actually caused harm.

Not only was Exxon prosecuted for generic offenses against "public" goods rather than for specific harms to specific parties, but the politicization of the spill resulted in a thoughtless policy response. Had a similar spill occurred in a more private setting—say, a tanker truck overturned, spilling onto private properties—the owners of the affected properties would have clear, direct recourse. Additionally, they would have a tangible incentive to ensure that any cleanup or remediation was a proper way to address the problem at hand.

Under current institutional arrangements, there was no means for affected citizens to hold Exxon directly responsible for much of the actual damage caused to the Alaskan shoreline. The Alaskan coast had no private owners, stewards, or protectors that could seek redress as if that oil had spilled into someone's backyard (or to ensure that cleanup dollars were well spent). The only direct payments made by Exxon to those actually harmed were to fishermen and Alaskan natives who claimed damages from a temporary decline in the salmon and seal harvest.[7]

If we truly want polluters to pay for the actual damages they cause, there need to be private property owners that can defend threatened or harmed resources. Ownership of ecological resources can serve as a deterrent against causing harm against others, in the same manner that private property provides such incentives in other areas. It also provides tangible incentives for better stewardship.[8]

Polluters such as Exxon should be held responsible not because they violated a bureaucratic proscription about the hunting of birds or harmed some "public" resource, but because they harmed someone else's person or property, and they have no right to do that. Any restitution should be paid to those harmed, not simply to a government agency that proclaims it will spend the money in the public interest.

A fishing club, the Pride of Derby, demonstrates how property rights can prevent stream pollution. In England, clubs own the right to fish along some rivers and thus are quick to respond to pollution threats. In 1948, several fishing-club members joined to form the Angler's Cooperative Association (ACA). In the Pride of Derby case, upstream polluters argued that their interests outweighed those of the club. Since the fishery was threatened, the club went to court and prevailed in protecting its riparian rights. The ACA has helped fishing clubs pursue injunctions against upstream pollution ever since. To date, the ACA has been involved in over 1,500 cases.[9]

This ability of private parties to restrain upstream polluters is rarely available in the United States. Historically, some communities had sought traditional common law remedies for interstate water pollution, which helped ensure that polluters paid. However, such actions have since been preempted by the federal Clean Water Act.[10] As with many environmental laws, whether or not someone is being harmed by an industrial activity is less important than whether the law is being followed. In some cases this leads to environmental overprotection, but it can lead to environmental underprotection as well. In either case, polluters are not held responsible for the actual wrongs they have committed.

Under the Clean Water Act, municipal polluters are treated preferentially. First, their cleanup goals are often less stringent than those of industrial polluters, and, second, they face far more lenient cleanup schedules. To politicians, the source of the pollution is as significant as the pollution itself. Politically-preferred polluters are treated more leniently than are pariah polluters. Yet, to the rivers and fish, pollution is pollution. If one believes that the polluter should pay, it should not matter who or what that polluter is.

This problem is compounded by the prevalence of citizen suit provisions in the Clean Water Act and other environmental laws. Under these provisions, private interest groups can effectively determine the enforcement priorities of government agencies. Due to the anti-business bias of many of the environmental organizations that engage in citizen suits, private industry is subject to more legal actions than either agricultural activities or governmental facilities, even though both are greater sources of water pollution. Indeed, between 1984 and 1988, environmentalist citizen suits against private industry were more than six times as common than suits against governmental facilities.[11] According to Michael Greve, "There are no *environmental* reasons why environmental groups would display such a pronounced preference for proceeding against corporate polluters."[12]

There is something profoundly unjust about limiting the legal recourse of persons harmed by polluting activities, while at the same time encouraging the use of citizen suits by organizations with no stake in the resources they claim to be protecting. Indeed, some environmental groups have found that citizen suits can be a lucrative source of revenue.[13]

Contentions to the contrary notwithstanding, today's environmental measures have very little to do with preventing pollution—they are not focused on preventing tangible harms to actual people and their properties. Both public and private enforcement have suffered from this tendency. If we accept the general principle that the polluter should pay, then we recognize that broad, drift-net emission-control strategies are ill-conceived. One size does not fit all. Forcing hundreds of small businesses to file extensive environmental reports makes little sense if the actions of only a few are causing environmental problems.

Drift-net approaches achieve pollution reductions more through their scope than their efficiency. As a result they tend to produce environmental improvements at the expense of innocent individuals who have not contributed to environmental harm. Even when the impacts of water- or air-borne emissions are extremely difficult to control, environmental protection and simple justice are better served when pollution reduction efforts focus on the true sources of pollution and ensure that it is the polluters that pay for the damages caused.

Consider the case of air pollution. It is well-established that a small fraction of automobiles are responsible for the vast preponderance of auto-related emissions. Indeed, over half of the emissions are generated by only 10 percent of the cars on the road.[14] This means that for every ten cars, the dirtiest one pollutes as much as the other nine. Nonetheless, federal officials insist upon imposing significant costs on the owners of all cars, through "clean fuel" requirements, periodic emissions inspections, and the like, in order to meet federal air quality standards. If additional emission reductions are necessary in some regions to protect human health (an arguable proposition), targeting the dirtiest portion of the automobile fleet will reduce pollution more efficiently—and more equitably as well. The majority of car owners whose vehicles are in clean-running condition should not be forced to pay for the pollution caused by an irresponsible minority. (Additionally, it is questionable whether the federal government should tell local communities what level of air emissions is acceptable; local officials are fully capable of making such decisions, and will be held accountable by local citizens.)

Some environmentalists and public officials suggest adopting the "polluter pays principle" through the imposition of emission taxes. This idea is generally associated with the economist A.C. Pigou, who argued that pollution taxes would force offending industries to "internalize" the costs they were imposing on others. There are two significant problems with this approach, however.

First, such taxes will be used to enrich government coffers, not to compensate those who are harmed by the pollution. It is one thing for the state to adjudicate disputes and ensure that polluters make restitution to those whom they have harmed. It is another thing for the state to identify polluting activities and use pollution taxes as a source of general revenue. The former is in accord with common law principles of justice; the latter encourages the continued growth of the regulatory state.

The second problem is that the state is in no position to assess the actual costs imposed by pollution. Pollution taxes enacted through the political process are likely to reflect political priorities, rather than environmental ones. The federal gasoline tax, for example, is often defended as a "polluter pays" approach because oil exploration, refining, and use all have environmental impacts. A tax on gasoline, however, is a poor proxy for taxing environmental impacts—the same gallon of gasoline will produce different levels of emissions in different vehicles. Furthermore, special-interest pleading will ensure that certain types of fuels and fuel additives receive special exemptions from the tax. Politically-derived taxes are always manipulated in this fashion and are no way to make the polluter pay.

A related problem is that pollution tax schemes almost inevitably rely upon some proxy for pollution in the assessment of the tax. This is true, generally, for so-called "pollution prevention" programs that are promoted by the Environmental Protection Agency. It is far easier to levy a tax on an easily measurable factor, such as use of a resource or aggregate emissions or waste generated, than it is to try and measure the impact upon people.

As already noted, not every emission, waste, discharge, or industrial by-product is pollution. Yet in the fervor to enact "pollution prevention" policies, environmental regulators adopt "waste reduction" and "toxics-use reduction" schemes. Such programs completely miss the point. The generation of waste, in and of itself, entails no necessary harm on other people or their property. Thus there is no reason for waste *per se* to be discouraged by government policy. Insofar as pollution-prevention efforts metastasize into crusades for the elimination of waste, they move away from any true concern for limiting pollution and holding polluters accountable for the damages that they cause.

Making the polluter pay should not entail trying to eliminate the generation of wastes and other by-products of a modern, industrial society. Nor does it mean regulating every emission, every industrial process, indeed every aspect of economic life. Rather, it means focusing environmental-protection efforts on the greatest sources of harm and ensuring that polluters pay for the costs of the harms they inflict upon others. This goal can be best accomplished through a decentralization of environmental policy and a greater reliance upon common law remedies. Central government dictates are not up to the task.

Zero-pollution is a laudable goal, but pollution prevention must mean the effort to eliminate the forcible imposition of environmental harms on other people and their property, not the elimination of all wastes, all emissions, or all industrial activities that environmental groups find distasteful. Properly defined, pollution control is coercion control. This is the essence of true environmental protection, and it should be the essence of American environmental policy.

Notes

1. It is important to separate "external harm"—harm that is involuntarily imposed by an outside actor—and harms that are the result of voluntary assumption of risk, such as results from a rock-climbing accident or engaging in unhealthy behavior.

2. See, for example, Sydney Howe, "Making the Polluters Pay," *Washington Post*, January 30, 1977.

3. US Environmental Protection Agency, *The Nation's Hazardous Waste Management Program at a Crossroads: The RCRA Implementation Study* (Washington, DC: US EPA, 1990), p. 36.

4. Marianne Lavelle, "Environmental Vise: Law, Compliance," *National Law Journal*, August 30, 1993, p. S1.

5. Jeff Berliner, "Exxon Pleads Guilty, Judge Accepts $1 Billion Settlement," United Press International, October 8, 1991.

6. "Oil Spill Money Creates New Alaska Park," Associated Press, May 27, 1994.

7. However, it should be noted that the jury awards to the fisherman were more likely the product of outrage over the spill than actual demonstrated damage; see Jeff Wheelwright, "Exxon Was Right, Alas," *New York Times*, July 31, 1994. This is another product of focusing on "public" harms rather than on harms inflicted on particular parties.

8. This point is elaborated in Robert J. Smith, "Resolving the Tragedy of the Commons by Creating Private Property Rights in Wildlife," *Cato Journal* (Fall 1981), pp. 439-468 [excerpt on pp. 101-110 of this volume].

9. This history is recounted in Kent Jeffreys, *Who Should Own the Ocean?* (Washington, DC: Competitive Enterprise Institute, 1991), pp. 17-18.

10. See Roger E. Meiners and Bruce Yandle, "Clean Water Legislation: Reauthorize or Repeal?" in *Taking the Environmental Seriously*, Meiners and Yandle, eds. (Lanham, Maryland: Rowman and Littlefield, 1993), pp. 88-94.

11. Michael Greve, "Private Enforcement, Private Rewards," in *Environmental Politics: Public Costs, Private Rewards*, M. Greve and F. Smith, eds. (New York: Praeger, 1992), p. 111.

12. Ibid.

13. Ibid., pp. 109-110.

14. J.G. Calvert, et al., "Achieving Acceptable Air Quality: Some Reflections on Controlling Vehicle Emission," *Science*, July 2, 1993, p. 40; and, Donald Stedman, et al., *On-Road Remote Sensing of CO and HC Emissions in California*, Final Report Contract No. A032-093 (Sacramento: California Air Resources Board, 1994), p. 13.

Free Trade Is Green Trade

James M. Sheehan

Environmentalist objections to trade and proposals for the "greening" of trade are a fundamental assault on free trade principles. They also threaten environmental quality. Free trade is essential for both wealth creation and environmental protection.

The Green Critique

"A more accurate name than the persuasive label 'free trade' is deregulated international commerce," scolds World Bank environmentalist Herman Daly.[1] International regulation of trade is necessary "to build environmental responsibility into economic activity,"[2] and to assure that "trade meets the goals of environmentally sustainable development,"[3] in the words of Jay Hair, president of one of the largest environmental organizations in the United States, the National Wildlife Federation. As trade has become globalized, environmentalists argue, so has the magnitude of environmental degradation. "Further growth beyond the present scale is overwhelmingly likely to increase costs more rapidly than it increases benefits, thus ushering in a new era of 'uneconomic growth' that impoverishes rather than enriches," the foreboding Daly intones.[4]

The "green" trade agenda necessarily entails greater political management and regulation of the private sector to safeguard social and environmental goals. In the eyes of environmental groups like the Worldwatch Institute, "trade can bring greater prosperity and improved quality of life, if properly managed, but if not it can

Excerpted from *The Greening of Trade Policy: "Sustainable Development" and Global Trade* (Washington, DC: Competitive Enterprise Institute, 1994).

become an engine of enormous destruction" of biodiversity, the global climate, and natural resources.[5] Fearing destruction of the "global" environment, environmental groups call for radical alterations in the free-market system by government.

Environmental activists are particularly concerned with trade between progressive nations (with high regulatory standards) and more free-market or less developed countries (with lower regulatory standards). Nations without strict regulatory standards attract accelerated flows of international capital investment, leading to the creation of "pollution havens."[6] The lack of stringent environmental regulation gives firms an unfair competitive trade advantage, amounting to an environmental subsidy which enables firms to undercut prices in export markets. This phenomenon is called environmental dumping, or "eco-dumping."[7] Vice President Al Gore, in his bestselling *Earth in the Balance*, argues that "weak and ineffectual enforcement of pollution control measures should also be included in the definition of unfair trading practices."[8]

The remedy for eco-dumping is a mixture of protectionism, industrial policy, and regulation. To offset the unfair cost advantages of another nation, a government can impose tariffs on the offending nation's imports (protectionism), or a government can subsidize the exports of its politically-preferred businesses (industrial policy).[9] The purpose of import and export restrictions and subsidies is to induce nations to adopt stricter environmental standards, "internalizing" the externalized costs of unenlightened environmental policies. In this manner, nations can "harmonize" their trade-related regulations and risk assessment practices to facilitate an overall improvement in standards.[10] Harmonization of production standards is envisioned as a means of establishing minimum environmental standards, either in the context of a regional trade agreement, or through a system of global environmental standards.[11]

Environmentalist opposition to free trade stems from harsh scrutiny of "market failure" and the uncritical acceptance of political approaches to environmental protection. Wherever the market "fails" to protect environmental values to the desired degree, political intervention is assumed to be the solution. Because all economic activities have some impact on environmental quality, there is no end in sight for government intervention in the marketplace.[12] Viewing economic growth as incompatible with a healthy environment, the environmental lobby insists on political restraints on private activity, both domestically and internationally. The environmentalist perspective is rapidly becoming conventional wisdom.

Richer Is Cleaner

Ultimately, however, there is no contradiction between a commercial free market and environmental quality. Numerous academic studies demonstrate a positive link between economic growth and environmental quality. Princeton University economists Gene M. Grossman and Alan B. Krueger have found that "economic growth tends to alleviate pollution problems once a country's per capita income reaches about $4,000 to $5,000 US dollars."[13] In fact, levels of sulfur dioxide are significantly lower in countries that engage in significant international trade.[14]

The link between economic growth and environmental improvement becomes clear in reviewing the ecological successes of the developed world. According to the World Bank, the economies of OECD countries have grown by approximately 80 percent since 1970.[15] During that time period, these countries have achieved nearly universal access to clean water supplies, sanitation, and waste disposal. Air quality has improved dramatically, with particulate emissions dropping by 60 percent and sulfur dioxide emissions by 38 percent. Pollution from large shipping accidents and oil spills has declined, and nearly all countries have increased the acreage of their forestlands. Similar statistics for the developing world demonstrate that improved environmental quality in all of these areas is generally associated with higher income.[16]

There are a variety of reasons for the beneficial relationship between growth and environmental quality. As economic activity increases, so does human interaction with nature. Since most human actions strive to improve quality of life, environmental amenities receive greater attention. Environmental improvements are particularly significant in market-oriented economies. The societal institutions that facilitate prosperity, such as property rights, market-based prices, and overall economic freedom, are equally essential for raising environmental quality. These institutions form the bulwark of private stewardship of natural resources and, thus, sustainable management practices. Market forces naturally drive economies to become more efficient by reducing the costs associated with energy and materials use, and waste disposal. Moreover, since growth creates wealth, greater economic resources are made available to address the primary human needs, which must be fulfilled before individuals will focus on environmental amenities. According to Marian Radetski, an economist at the University of Luleo in Sweden, "rich consumers are more willing than poor ones to spend substantial parts of their income for safeguarding high environmental standards."[17]

Furthermore, poverty is a significant cause of environmental degradation. Poorer people are more likely to exploit environmental commons in search of fuelwood and other basic necessities, causing overhunting, overfishing, and stress to water resources.[18] Lacking significant employment opportunities and productive land, the poor in the Third World often must utilize marginal lands for food production, attempting to farm in deserts or tropical forests. The result is environmental degradation in the form of soil erosion, desertification, and deforestation.[19]

Moreover, economic growth enables societies to advance in ways that are environmentally beneficial. At earlier stages of development, pollution problems are likely to be more threatening to human beings. Air- and water-borne hazards can result in immediate illness or death. As societies advance, pollution problems decline in severity. Environmental concerns generally become less life-threatening, and more aesthetic in nature.

Even though growth coincides with environmental improvement, "market failure" is often blamed for the existence of pollution itself. Many environmentalists consider the system of capitalism and private enterprise inherently responsible for environmental externalities. Only government regulation in the public interest can force businesses to internalize social costs, according to this argument, and such regulation must be extended to trade. Thus, there is a strong anti-market bias to environmentalist arguments.

The market-failure argument leads inexorably to central planning; any human activity with environmental impacts must be politically controlled. Government is entrusted to effectively foster only the types of economic growth which are environmentally friendly, while preventing the types that are not. Yet no government has the capability of assimilating the vast amounts of economic, technological, and scientific data necessary to make such determinations. The task of ecological central planning is no easier than economic central planning.[20]

If market failure was truly the cause of pollution, we would expect the absence of markets in the centrally-planned economies of Eastern Europe would have been environmentally beneficial. On the contrary, without the profit motive of the market, some of the worst environmental degradation in the world occurred in the former Soviet Bloc.[21] Central planning failed largely because it could not efficiently distribute resources. Neither could it safeguard environmental resources. Data from sample market and socialist economies shows that market economies become more resource-efficient with economic growth. Socialist countries, however, are generally more resource intensive, even in times of recession.[22] Without a profit motive, there is little incentive for political owners of a resource to conserve for the future in order to maximize returns.[23]

James M. Sheehan

Free Markets Are Truly Green

In a market economy, environmental and other costs are internalized more thoroughly via the price system. Internalization is made possible by the extension of property rights and a system of voluntary exchange to an ever-wider array of resources. As environmental and other resources are integrated into the market system of voluntary exchange, information is conveyed through prices, which encourages more creative resolutions of environmental and other problems. Falling prices for energy and raw materials demonstrate that the market's technological improvements and efficiency gains are making resources more abundant.[24]

The "market failure" argument misses the fundamental cause of pollution—the lack of private property institutions. Individuals are far more likely to care for the environmental sustainability of their own resources. Logically, the less common property there is, the less pollution will be tolerated by a society of individual property owners. Likewise, by internalizing external costs, market forces obviate the need for corrective regulations. By reducing the scope of government intervention, markets enable individuals to seek redress from those who impose unwanted pollution costs. Political owner/managers are incapable of seeking adequate redress primarily because they cannot calculate accurate prices and values for environmental amenities.[25] Thus, a free market effectively implements the "polluter pays principle," making capitalism the only form of sustainable development.[26] Pollution externalities could be reduced further by eliminating the remaining barriers to full private property rights.

Environmentalists need not fear that expansion of trade will produce growth in pollution. To the extent that expanded trade is generating economic growth, environmental quality should also improve. This fundamental economic reality does not change simply because goods and services are crossing borders. The same free-market institutions which generate economic gains also generate environmental gains. To the extent that protective tariffs and subsidies restrict and distort trade, they reduce income and, hence, the demand for environmental quality.

Environmentalists have more to fear from protectionism. Current agricultural policies cause major distortions of world food production and trade.[27] Industrial countries encourage agricultural production with price supports and other subsidies totaling $200 billion per year, while developing countries discourage agricultural production through tax and trade policies.[28] Agricultural subsidies in the United States, for example, are responsible for intense chemical pesticide and fertilizer use on farmlands. By fostering inefficient land use, US subsidies and land set-aside programs contribute to soil erosion and loss of wetlands and forests. Federal mismanagement also encourages farmers to overplant while discouraging crop rotation, depleting soils and exacerbating pest eradication.[29] By scaling back interventionist government policies, trade liberalization would have significant environmental benefits.

Notes

1. Herman Daly, "The Perils of Free Trade," *Scientific American* (November 1993).

2. Jay D. Hair, "GATT and the Environment," *Journal of Commerce*, December 8, 1993.

3. Testimony of Jay D. Hair, president of the National Wildlife Federation, before the Senate Committee on Commerce, Subcommittee on Trade and Environmental Issues, February 3, 1994.

4. Herman Daly and John B. Cobb, Jr., *For the Common Good: Redirecting the Economy Toward Community, the Environment, and a Sustainable Future* (Boston: Beacon Press, 1989), p. 2.

5. Hilary F. French, "Costly Tradeoffs: Reconciling Trade and the Environment," *Worldwatch Paper*, no. 113 (Worldwatch Institute, March 1993), p. 9.

6. Ibid., p. 29.

7. Robert Repetto, "Trade and Environmental Policies: Achieving Complimentarities and Avoiding Conflicts," *Issues and Ideas* (New York: World Resources Institute, 1993), p. 5.

8. Al Gore, *Earth in the Balance* (New York: Houghton Mifflin, 1992), p. 343.

9. Charles Arden-Clarke, "The General Agreement on Tariffs and Trade, Environmental Protection and Sustainable Development," World Wildlife Fund Discussion Paper, June 1991, p. 1.

10. Repetto, "Trade and Environmental Policies," p. 6.

11. French, "Costly Tradeoffs," p. 35-36.

12. See Fred L. Smith, Jr., "Environmental Quality, Economic Growth, and International Trade" (Washington, DC: Competitive Enterprise Institute, 1992).

13. Gene M. Grossman and Alan B. Krueger, "Environmental Impacts of a North American Free Trade Agreement" (Princeton: Princeton University, 1991), p. 35.

14. Ibid., p. 17.

15. World Bank, *World Development Report 1992: Development and the Environment* (New York: Oxford University Press, 1992), p. 40.

16. Ibid., p. 11.

17. Marian Radetzki elaborates on the market's incentives for environmental protection; "Economic Growth and the Environment," *Symposium on International Trade and the Environment*, International Trade Division, International Economics Department (World Bank, November 21-22, 1991), p. 22.

18. *World Resources, 1992-93* (New York: World Resources Institute, 1992), pp. 30-31.

19. Ibid.

20. See Fred L. Smith, Jr., "The Market and Nature," *The Freeman* (September 1993) [see pages 25-38 in this volume].

21. Thomas DiLorenzo, "Does Capitalism Cause Pollution?" *Contemporary Issues Series*, no. 38 (Center for the Study of American Business, August 1990).

22. Mikhail S. Bernstam, "The Wealth of Nations and the Environment" (London: Institute of Economic Affairs, 1991).

23. Thomas DiLorenzo, "The Mirage of Sustainable Development," *The Futurist* (September/October 1993).

24. *World Development Report 1992*, p. 37.

25. Daniel C. Esty, *Greening the GATT: Trade, Environment, and the Future* (Washington, DC: Institute for International Economics, 1994), pp. 66-67. Esty criticizes markets for not "getting environmental prices right" but admits that there is no agreed method for political calculation of prices.

26. See Roger E. Meiners and Bruce Yandle, *Taking the Environment Seriously* (Boston: Rowman & Littlefield Publishers, 1993).

27. GATT Secretariat, "Trade and the Environment," Final Report: International Trade 90-91, vol. 1 (General Agreement on Tariffs and Trade, February 3, 1992), pp. 32-35.

28. Dennis Avery, *World Food Progress 1991* (Indianapolis: Hudson Institute Center for Global Food Issues, 1991), pp. 172-177.

29. Ibid., p. 216. Also see Richard L. Stroup and Jane S. Shaw, "Environmental Harms from Federal Government Policy," in Meiners and Yandle, *Taking the Environment Seriously*, pp. 51-72.

Superfund
A Hazardous Waste of Taxpayer Money

Fred L. Smith, Jr.

House and Senate conferences are nearing agreement on a $8.5 billion, five-year reauthorization of the Superfund law (the Comprehensive Environmental Response, Compensation and Liability Act of 1980). Such a massive expansion of federal toxic-waste cleanup efforts promises to unleash the largest pork-barrel program in history, expend great sums to little result, and preempt more effective solutions to the problems posed by abandoned chemical dumps.

If this bill is enacted, the Reagan Administration will largely be to blame. The Environmental Protection Agency (EPA) and the White House have been remarkably feeble in challenging the hysterical, zero-risk, anti-business, technology-fearing advocates of this legislation. Instead, they have retreated into a defensive shell. Rather than opposing the waste cleanup legislation as bad environmental policy—regardless of its pricetag—White House officials have argued for a lower reauthorization increase(from the current $1.6 to $5.3 rather than $8.5 billion) and have quibbled over the proposal to finance Superfund with a new, broad-based business tax.

In addition, the Administration has provided conflicting signals to Congress—threatening to veto if the funding level, tax problems, and liability rules aren't corrected, while simultaneously allowing the EPA to send Congress a threatening letter of the "We're going to close the Washington Monument" variety unless new

Excerpted from *Human Events*, August 2, 1986. Reprinted with permission.

legislation is soon enacted. Its inconsistencies and failure to challenge the overall program have once again made it easy to caricature the Administration as an anti-environmental, pro-business penny-pincher standing in the way of congressional defenders of American health and safety.

Enactment of this bill would provide dramatic evidence of the failure of the Administration to develop any coherent approach to environmental policy. As detailed below, the Administration knows full well that:

(1) Superfund stems from a total misreading of the Love Canal incident (a situation where private protections were thwarted by public mismanagement);

(2) The magnitude of health risks addressed by Superfund are small to nonexistent;

(3) The legislation contains few features designed to target funds to the more significant cleanup sites;

(4) The liability provisions encourage a "no-fault" concept that undermines the basic principle that polluters—not the innocent taxpayer—should pay pollution costs;

(5) The new taxes embodied in this bill constitute a serious threat to the business commodity; and

(6) The bill will preempt far more effective solutions to the problems posed by hazardous wastes.

For these reasons, the Administration should veto the proposed Superfund reauthorization bill, accept a short-term interim extension of the program, and seek aggressively to reframe the Superfund debate in the 100th Congress. Environmental policy is far too important to be transformed into another public works boondoggle.

Origins of Superfund: Love Canal "Disaster"

Superfund from its beginning has been little more than a Superfraud. Launched in 1980 as a hastily concocted response to the Love Canal incident, the program is founded upon erroneous assumptions about the cause and nature of the hazardous waste threat.

Love Canal was an area around Buffalo in which the Hooker Chemical Co. had once discarded toxic chemical wastes. As chemical substances from the waste disposal site began to leach into the water table and infiltrate the soil in the surrounding residential community, the national media learned of the event and the "Love Canal Disaster" was born.

EPA leadership seized upon this incident to garner political support for their then-languishing Superfund legislative proposal. The EPA contracted for a "quickie" medical survey, which appeared to show increased health risks for Love Canal residents, and released these results at an "emergency" press conference covered by all the major television networks.

Americans were bombarded with powerful media images of oozing, noxious chemicals juxtaposed with nervous, concerned families. Love Canal and "chemical threats to your health" became national concerns and Superfund was approved by Congress.

Moreover, Hooker Chemical seemed the perfect corporate villain, with its "no comment" response to the adverse publicity. Once more (so it appeared), a private firm motivated only by short-term profits had sought to economize by dumping deadly waste on an innocent and unsuspecting citizenry. The market having failed, so went the argument, the Superfund Act should be implemented as swiftly as possible.

As detailed in an investigative story by the Reason Foundation ("Love Canal: The Truth Seeps Out"), and as was known at the time to EPA, Hooker Chemical had no direct control over or responsibility for the incident. In 1953, Hooker was forced, under the threat of eminent domain, to deed over the site to the local school board, which wanted the land for a new school.

Hooker protested the land transfer. It argued that a hazardous waste disposal site was no place for a school. The company gave way only after further pressure from local officials and acknowledgment in the deed transfer document that the school board had been warned of the chemical wastes buried on the site.

At the time of the transfer, Hooker had taken considerable care in disposing of its waste materials. The company placed them in a clay-lined trench (the former canal) which was capped with an additional four feet of clay. Today, such a landfill would probably receive EPA operating approval. Hooker undertook such relatively expensive precautions because, as a private property owner, it feared eventual damage claims if its waste ever came into contact with third parties.

Thus, private ownership of a potential hazard in a litigious society seemed to perform exactly as we might hope—a private party acted in a publicly responsible manner to protect its own self-interest.

On the other hand, the local school board politics of Niagara Falls—as "public servants"—had few concerns about being sued and thus felt free to ignore any problems their carelessness might create.

Thus, the board began its school, but soon found declining school populations required less land than originally anticipated. Acting more like stereotypical rapacious capitalists than disinterested public servants, the board sought to sell the remaining land (including the dump site itself) to a residential developer. Despite Hooker's repeated warnings that the site contained potentially life-threatening materials and should not be used for residential housing, the board eventually found a local realtor unaware of the controversy and swiftly transferred the hot potato to him.

Unlike Hooker, neither the school board nor the unaware new owner concerned themselves with preserving the integrity of the landfill. Much of the clay cap was scraped away, at first during construction of the school and then again for the housing develop-ment. Sewers and roads to serve the latter were allowed to be built through the site itself. All these activities eventually combined to allow the buried hazardous materials to leach from the disposal site into the surrounding water table, thereby triggering the Love Canal "disaster" story.

The real facts of Love Canal contradict the "evil capitalist" myth. When a private company (Hooker) owned the property, it was seriously concerned about the long-term consequences of its activities, and justifiably so, since it expected to be around for many decades and was fully aware of potential legal claims that could be brought against the firm. On the other hand, political officials obsessed with the short run (holding down tax assessments) and having little concern over possible financial liability proved irresponsible guardians of public safety.

The neglected lesson of Love Canal is that it actually showed how private property rights encourage consideration of low-probability, long-range risks. But the "conclusions" promoted by Superfund advocates and the national media were that the free market had failed to handle the hazardous waste threat and a major new federal program was essential.

The Health Hoax

Love Canal convinced Americans that hazardous waste dumps posed a serious health risk and required an immediate, emergency response. Yet follow-up studies at Love Canal turned up no evidence of abnormal levels of morbidity or mortality.

For example, a distinguished panel of scientists appointed by New York Governor Hugh Carey reported in October, 1980, that "there has been no demonstration of acute health effects linked to exposure to hazardous wastes at the Love Canal site. The panel has also concluded that chronic effects of hazardous waste exposure at Love Canal have neither been established nor ruled out yet."

A study by the New York State Department of Health published in the journal *Science* in June, 1981, concluded, "Data from the New York Cancer Registry show no evidence for higher cancer rates associated with residence near the Love Canal toxic waste burial site in comparison with the entire state outside of New York City." In June, 1983, the Center for Disease Control (CDC) noted no excess illness among persons living close to the Love Canal. Another CDC report in March, 1984, found "no increase in the frequency of chromosomal abnormalities of residents in the Love Canal area."

The hysteria and political pressures that have led to the rapid expansion of Superfund reflect an extremely successful effort to repackage a traditional pork-barrel program as a human-health and cancer-preventive measure. Superfund defenders have convinced a lot of Americans that we are dealing with emergency situations and any effort to correct the program's problems will intolerably slow down urgent cleanup efforts. Unfortunately, such voodoo environmentalism remains largely unchallenged.

For many hundreds of years, mankind has produced waste materials that, if improperly handled, could create health problems and reduce the quality of the environment. The early dye works involved noxious chemicals, as did the alchemist shops of the Middle Ages. Superfund is predicated on the belief that this hazardous waste problem has reached crisis proportions and now poses an unusually severe risk to human health and the environment. The Superfund program embodies a sense of urgency in which normal requirements of proof and cost-benefit analysis are suspended. The house is on fire and there is no time for careful consideration.

Yet we really know little about the quality of underground water in the United States, and even less about the actual health hazards that might arise from toxic waste dumps. Six years after Love Canal, we still don't know which toxic materials in what doses are dangerous to human beings, nor whether these dosages are likely to occur given groundwater flows and normal countermeasures.

Evidence that hazardous materials in dump sites have migrated into groundwater and damaged human health has been difficult to produce. The original Superfund legislation charged the Department of Health and Human Services with investigating such toxic health hazards, but little has been done (in keeping with a long tradition of self-ignorance directing federal environmental policy).

The health threat of greatest salience in fueling reflexive support for Superfund is cancer, which accounts for about one-fourth of all deaths in the United States. But according to the best estimates now available, lifestyle factors such as smoking, diet, and sunshine exposure account for the overwhelming portion of all cancer fatalities.

The small fraction of cancers attributable to man-made chemicals via all modes of exposure—both workplace and environmental—is perhaps 6 percent. Since the levels of exposure are likely to be far higher in occupational settings, there is little evidence to date that environmental levels of contamination are at all linked to human cancer.

Even using a common estimate that about 1 percent of all cancer can be traced to environmental pollution, one must recognize that such a figure includes pollution from airborne carcinogens, from surface contaminants, from food additives, from pesticide residuals, and other sources. Only a fraction of such risks can be associated with groundwater contamination. Superfund thus addresses a tiny speck of the cancer problem in the United States.

Moreover, there are no data that cancers caused by man-made substances are increasing. Epidemiological evidence, of course, cannot absolutely rule out the possibility of future risks from man-made substances; however, existing data coupled with the lack of any evidence of higher cancer incidence in Europe (where hazardous chemicals have a much longer history) suggest any such risk is small. Indeed, growing research indicates that mankind actually lives, and has lived for thousands of years, in the midst of many natural carcinogenic materials. The argument that human beings are at risk primarily from novel, man-made chemicals (appealing to nostalgic fanciers of pre-industrial society) now appears to be dead wrong.

Since the human health benefits from Superfund appear small, the case for a massive federal program in this area must rely on its value in protecting vital groundwater supplies. Certainly, some wastes are leaching into some aquifers which somewhat reduces their utility and such damages should be disciplined. However, here as elsewhere, data are extremely limited on the extent to which aquifers are actually threatened. There is certainly no evidence that hazardous wastes are a major or even significant threat in comparison to other factors endangering this vital resource: excessive depletion (allowing saltwater contamination, for example), government-subsidized water supply (encouraging waste), government-subsidized development (threatening water sheds), and the inefficient ownership rights which make it difficult for individuals to manage this resource privately.

Even in the area of contamination, the major health risk continues to be "natural" bacterial and viral contamination of water supplies, rather than chemical waste contamination. These risks are managed in a decentralized fashion, with each water supplier and each individual well user taking precautions directly. Nonetheless, there is no federal Sanitary Waste Superfund dedicated to digging up abandoned outhouses throughout the United States. (At least not yet.)

Hazardous Waste Cleanup: Political Growth Industry

Despite the deliberate misreading of the Love Canal incident and its human health consequences, Congress rapidly enacted the Superfund legislation to address "emergency" cleanup situations and orphan dumps and provided an initial funding of $1.6 billion. The program promised to make hazardous wastes "go away" at no cost to local communities. The federal government pays 90 per cent, and the state picks up the remaining expense. To the local citizenry, Superfund is a "free good" of all benefits and no burden. Naturally, the program has become extremely popular.

The number of sites "needing" attention has increased from the initial 400 priority sites (about one for every congressional district) to the EPA's current estimate of 2,000 such locations. Superfund's sponsors further encouraged this feeding frenzy by avoiding any clear definition of starting or stopping rules in addressing risk management responsibilities, site selection, and determination of appropriate cleanup strategies.

The Superfund Act provides very little guidance on how serious threats are to be distinguished from mere nuisances. Under Superfund, hazards include any materials that are flammable (e.g. charcoal lighters), toxic (insecticides), corrosive (Clorox or Oven Off), or reactive (Drano)—or any substances that the EPA designates as hazardous. Moreover, the legislation suggests and the EPA has adopted a definition of "hazardous" that gives considerable weight to extremely unlikely situations. If something *might* happen, Superfund assumes it *will* happen. Under this worse case analysis, too many sites are classified as "hazardous" even though, as noted above, the evidence suggests that the overall human risk associated with all chemical wastes is low.

Since Superfund fails to target the most serious problems, the EPA finds itself selecting projects based on their political and public relations value. In case after case, the EPA has rushed to spend money for "cleanups" where the threat to health has been low to non-existent or where responsibility could obviously be assigned. In Times Beach, Missouri, for example, the EPA purchased all the homes in the area for $30 million on the basis of studies finding dioxin contamination of soil in the area. Experimental animal studies do show dioxin to be extremely toxic; however, as is often the case, animals respond differently from humans, and there is no evidence that any humans have ever suffered any chronic health problem from exposure to this substance. That finding is based on epidemiological studies of industrial accidents in which exposures have been many times those encountered at Times Beach. Elizabeth Whelan in her book *Toxic Terrors* noted, "Times Beach, like Love Canal, is an environmental problem turned into an environmental fiasco. Decisions and subsequent actions were based as much on political considerations as on public health realities." A recent *Science American* article on the dioxin scare noted,

> What [the EPA] has not done—and might be said to
> have a responsibility to do—is to try to dispel the
> public's fear on the basis of the evidence that exposure to low concentrations of TCDD (dioxin) in the
> environment appears *not* to have a serious chronic
> effect on human beings.

The EPA *might* have taken such prudent actions, but given the value of scare tactics to an expanding Superfund budget, we can understand why it did not.

Superfund has also encouraged communities to seek federal funding rather than go after responsible parties. After all, the program was originally intended to clean up a small number of "abandoned, orphan" sites. However, as the Love Canal incident indicates, the EPA has made Superfund monies available whenever penalizing the real polluters (the public officials in that case) would be politically difficult. As a result, Superfund's "priority" list now includes a number of sites operated by viable companies and even by the Department of Defense.

The "worst case" criterion for risk assessment also encourages the EPA to add low-risk sites to the Superfund program. James Bovard, an investigative journalist, identifies one site, an inactive city dump in Windom, Minnesota, that was closed in 1974. As one would expect, the wells on site were indeed contaminated, but Bovard notes that the EPA found that off-site municipal and residential wells were not. Nonetheless, the site was added to the "priority" list. Bovard notes, "If finding of non-contamination justifies adding this site to the Superfund list, why wouldn't every past and present city dump in the US be included?"

❖　❖　❖

Feeding Fund's Appetite: Search for Deep Pockets

Although the political popularity of Superfund has resulted in major pressures to increase funding, finding ways to finance such demands has delayed final congressional reauthorization of the program.

The initial funding sources for Superfund—taxes levied on the standard pariahs of American industry, the oil and chemical industries, and recoveries from "responsible parties," again largely oil and chemical companies—have been stressed by demands encouraged by this legislation. As a result, Congress has begun to consider new revenue sources.

Until recently, House conferees insisted upon increasing taxes on the oil and chemical industries while Senate conferees sought a broad-based tax on manufacturers, similar to a national value-added tax (VAT). Concern over the uncompetitive status of the financially strapped oil and chemical industries finally seems to have won out over the desire of many House members to bleed them dry. As a result, there is basic agreement upon using a broad-based business-profits tax to supplement the existing oil and chemical tax.

But the inequity of the initial Superfund burden on the oil and chemical sector (why should anyone be singled out to address the problems of "orphan" dumps?) should not blind one to the equally inequitable decision to address pollution problems by taxing everybody from ice cream to furniture manufacturers. Two wrongs don't make a right, and singling out any group of innocent parties and imposing on them the costs of cleaning up the pollution created by someone else is bad public policy.

Enactment of any new broad-based revenue measure, even on a limited basis, is akin to introducing a tactical nuclear weapon into a conventional war. Once unleashed, this seemingly "painless" taxation almost certainly will rapidly increase. It threatens uncontrollable escalation of the tax burden. Imagine the combination of Superfund's unquenchable thirst for popular pork-barrel projects with such a renewable revenue source—the fiscal equivalent of an out-of-control breeder reactor!

Defining "Responsibility" Irresponsibly

Part of Superfund's cleanup expenses, of course, are supposed to be financed by those parties "responsible" for creating hazardous waste problems. The Superfund Act required the EPA to identify such parties—no easy task in the case of what are, after all, supposed to be abandoned sites. But Superfund officials simply eliminated in practice any normal usage of the term "responsibility" from decisions as to who is to be held "responsible."

The program treats as a responsible party anyone who has any economic connection with the dumpsite. If a company is found to have deposited a single barrel of waste at a dumpsite, it can be held liable for all site cleanup costs. These rules make the jobs of EPA and Justice Department lawyers easier, at the sacrifice of fairness and efficiency. In a recent hearing, an EPA enforcement lawyer noted that the legal-responsibility standards now prevailing under Superfund have largely eliminated all arguments about guilt and innocence. The focus of attention is on who can pay.

A high-ranking EPA official recently admitted that the program was custom-made to go after big oil and chemical companies. Superfund's loose interpretation to joint-and-several-liability makes it all too easy and all too tempting to prosecute wealthier firms, rather than the most responsible parties. But trying to impose legal responsibility on parties who feel they have done nothing wrong can create costs of its own—resistance in the form of lengthy litigation which delays actual cleanup operations and may actually exceed the latter's cost.

In practice, Superfund's liability rules make every party involved with hazardous wastes—the original source, the transporter, the site operator—potentially liable. Spreading the blame over such a wide range of individual parties not only diffuses responsibility, it also undermines safety incentives. After all, if individual actions can do little to reduce liability, there is little reason to adopt risk-reduction measures. Why bother if your ultimate responsibility is determined largely by the acts of others outside your control?

Superfund abandons the "Polluter Pays" principle (the costs of pollution should be borne by the polluter) in favor of a "Deep Pocket" theory of justice. This approach may make it easier to recover revenues in the short run. But the move towards a "no-fault" pollution policy drastically weakens incentives for individual parties to adopt less-polluting policies over time. Profitable "tax" policy isn't good environmental policy.

Insurers Beware

The heavy legal club created by Superfund may well put the fear of God into accused parties, but it almost certainly causes more harm than good. The unlimited liability that might fall upon anyone associated with a waste site has seriously damaged the insurance market for hazardous waste manufacturers, transporters, and the disposers. In the late 1970s, several private companies had sprung up to provide such parties with liability insurance coverage, and to encourage more effective hazardous waste management techniques. But with the onset of Superfund's megaliability threat, the insurers ran to the hills.

If the private insurance business for these risks had been allowed to develop we would have seen far more progress in procedures to gauge the risk of various waste-handling techniques. Private insurers would have had every incentive to spend the money to find out exactly what the dangers were. Their efforts would have nicely supplemented the EPA's work. Thanks to the revenue-hungry, joint-and-several-liability approach of Superfund, we wind up with neither private insurance nor the market-based regulation that it could provide.

Superfund Needs Rethinking, Not Reauthorization

The Superfund "debate" has barely moved beyond the proposition that hazardous wastes are potentially harmful and therefore more federal spending is necessary. But Congress, having learned little from its past environmental policy failures, should not be allowed to write another blank check to pursue an undefined concept of cleanliness. To sustain a veto of the reauthorization measure likely to come out of conference later this month, the Reagan Administration must seriously fight the Superfund steamroller on environmental, not just fiscal, grounds. It must make clear that although sharing the stated goals of Superfund's patrons, it finds serious problems in their means.

Strategically, the Administration must use the time wisely to come to grips with its greatest weakness in environmental policy— its failure to develop a market-oriented environmental policy. In the Superfund area, this means taking off the green eyeshades and arguing boldly for more imaginative, less intrusive alternatives to address the problems posed by hazardous dumps, primarily the protection of the nation's groundwater supplies. Developing an adequate strategy will take time; however, it would include reorganizing aquifer property rights, "labeling" of suspect site materials to ensure self-identifying of contamination, and reconsideration of other governmental policies (pricing, subsidies, conservation) which affect water quality.

More than five years into the "Reagan Revolution," it's time to stop running for cover on the environmental front and start taking the offensive.

Owning the Unownable

Paul Georgia

One of the most fascinating intellectual debates since the calculation debate over socialism in the 1930s is now raging in the environmental arena. The debate is over the most effective means of protecting the environment: government control or private stewardship. I call this debate the stewardship debate.

The arguments that Ludwig von Mises and F.A. Hayek used in the calculation debate are an important part of the current stewardship debate. The issues they raised—the knowledge problem and the role of market prices and private ownership—are an integral part of the intellectual arsenal used by advocates of ecological privatization.

Indeed, the dynamics of the stewardship debate mirror in many ways the calculation debate. Until Mises fired the first shot, socialists shrewdly avoided the economic feasibility of socialism by merely asserting the superiority of socialism over capitalism. To them it was sufficient to show the weaknesses of capitalism and, having done so, proclaim that socialism was the logical and inevitable outcome. Because markets failed to produce utopian results, socialism was declared the appropriate path to societal betterment.

Mises, however, argued that without the signals that market prices provide, economic calculation is impossible—that is, producers cannot know what to produce, how much to produce, and how to produce it efficiently. Under socialism, producers would be blind to the wants of consumers because socialism lacked prices.

Originally appeared in *The Freeman*, March 1995.

Without market prices we are left with a system of "groping about in the dark."[1]

The socialists eventually conceded prices mattered, but still claimed markets and private property were not necessary. They argued central planners could overcome the problem of calculation by simulating market prices through mathematical and statistical models.

Hayek ultimately defeated this "market socialist" argument by pointing out that arriving at realistic prices would require an enormous amount of information, and the knowledge necessary for such an undertaking is dispersed and fragmentary, frustrating any attempt at consolidation.[2] Israel Kirzner later stated that not only would the planners lack the necessary information but they would be ignorant of their own ignorance.[3] No mind or group of minds could possibly contain the necessary information needed for such a task.[4]

The stewardship debate has followed a similar progression. Private property advocates have made powerful theoretical and empirical arguments to show the superiority of private stewardship and markets over government-directed environmental protection. Many environmentalists have essentially conceded this point. They have agreed (in word if not in deed) that markets and private property create powerful incentives which lead to more effective and efficient environmental protection.

However, they say, this is only true where property rights are easily defined and exchanged. In other areas, defining property rights appears nearly impossible. For example, Robert Stavins, an environmental economist, promotes "economic-incentive mechanisms" that allow trades of pollution rights, but only after pollution goals have been established politically. These mechanisms, Stavins says, encourage efficiency but "avoid the impracticalities of the pure, private-property approach." He asks scornfully, "Does anybody really believe acid rain can be efficiently controlled by assigning property rights for the US airshed and then effecting negotiations among all affected parties?"[5]

Unfortunately, many who advocate market solutions fail to address this question. They acquiesce under the daunting task of defining property rights in such areas as airsheds, ground water, and oceans.[6] But it is important that free market environmentalists take on these more difficult issues.

There are essentially three arguments advanced by critics of free market environmentalism. The first is that it is impossible to assign property rights to, or "fence," the atmosphere, groundwater, or the oceans. Indeed, "fencing" the airshed, groundwater or oceans appears difficult, but so did the fencing of the Western frontier of the United States in the 19th century. At first, land was plentiful and there was no need to clearly define property rights. However, over time, land became more scarce and therefore more valuable. The higher value spurred greater efforts to fence the frontier and to more clearly define property rights.

But wood was scarce in the arid West and the distances to be fenced were enormous. Various solutions evolved, as Terry Anderson and P.J. Hill have shown. For example, camp lines were used to keep cattle herds separate; these "human fences" were effective but the costs of such methods were high. Eventually, the invention of a simple technology—barbed wire—greatly reduced the costs of delineating and protecting property rights.[7]

So, property rights do evolve. However, framing the issue in such terms as "fencing the airshed" is misleading. It is not necessary to fence and assign property rights to the atmosphere to reduce pollution. What is necessary is the existence of clearly defined and binding property rights to pollution-causing activities, as well as to the properties that are affected by the pollution. In a system of clearly defined and effectively protected property rights, the value of clean air and other environmental amenities will be revealed.

Before discussing how these preferences will emerge, an important distinction must be made between pollution and emissions or waste. Waste is simply a by-product of human action. Every productive and useful human action, even eating, creates waste. However, waste is not by definition pollution. Only when waste is dumped where it is not wanted (i.e., on another's property) does it become pollution. Property owners have the right to restrict the dumping of waste on their property whether it is in the airspace or the property itself.

In a property-rights based society, individuals will have the ability to sue for redress when their property rights are trespassed. If the property owner is successful the polluting firm must find ways to keep emissions from traveling onto another's land. However, if a firm wishes to continue to pollute, and property rights are clearly defined, it can purchase the right to do so from the property owner. By allowing property owners to negotiate among themselves, the value of clean air can emerge through the revealed prices, and the optimal amount of pollution will be achieved.[8] Moreover, private ownership creates incentives to develop more effective means of protecting property rights through technological advances.

At this point, environmentalists bring up their second argument, the problem of transaction costs. Even if rights are clearly defined it is too costly, they say, for thousands of people affected by automobile pollution to get together with thousands of car drivers and negotiate a mutually satisfying agreement. The enormous amount of time needed just to reach a consensus among such a large number of individuals is only one of the prohibitive costs involved in such an undertaking.

However, just as technology solved the fencing problem in the American West, it may do so for pollution. For example, technology developed at the University of Denver allows the measurement of automobile emissions as a car travels similar to the way radar measures speed. Stationary emission checkpoints along the highway can measure the amount of exhaust an automobile discharges as it travels. If the car exceeds the maximum limit, a photograph of the license plate is taken and the person pays a fine.

Most people see this technology as a more efficient means for the government to control pollution by catching those who drive the dirtiest automobiles.[9] But to those who think more deeply, this new technology provides a means of reducing the transaction costs while expanding freedom.

Highways—not just airsheds—could be privatized. Those who wish to negotiate for cleaner air only have to deal with one entity, the highway owner. Instead of thousands of homeowners attempting to negotiate with thousands of automobile users, there is an owner of a segment of highway negotiating with perhaps ten, twenty-five or fifty homeowner associations. (Such associations could address these environmental concerns just as they have addressed crime and a range of other common landowner interests).

The highway owner, using the new emission detection device, could charge user fees, fines, or outright prohibition against highway use to automobiles that pollute excessively, exposing the highway owner to potential liability.

As the costs of such negotiations decrease, the amount of pollution will approach a level that everyone will be happy with. Either the highway owner can pay the home associations to be allowed to pollute, or the home associations can pay the highway user to reduce pollution. If the highway owner exceeds the stipulated amount the home associations can sue for damages. Either way an optimal amount of pollution is more nearly approached.[10] In an environment free from government interference, private institutions can evolve (perhaps slowly), leading to optimal solutions. Technology acts as a catalyst through which the costs of enforcing property rights are greatly reduced.

This system also allows time- and place-appropriate solutions. In Los Angeles, clean air is scarce. In Idaho it is plentiful. Although transaction costs and the costs of defining property rights over previously unowned resources may be the same in both places, Los Angeles will be more likely, in the absence of government interference, to undertake the necessary market transactions because Los Angelenos will value clean air more than Idahoans.

Under centralized control, Idahoans would pay the same for clean air as those in Los Angeles even though they don't value it as much. Thus, transaction costs are overcome in two ways; first, new technologies can greatly reduce transaction costs, and second, the value of clean air may be high enough to exceed the transaction costs of negotiating a solution.[11]

Of course, people may not want a cleaner environment so much that they are willing to pay for the necessary technology or transaction costs. In strict economic terms, this means that at the current costs of pollution reduction, people only demand a certain level of clean air. Those who aren't satisfied with the amount of clean air achieved through the market go to government to force the rest of us to pay more for clean air than we want to. Since the costs of politically-managed clean air are hidden, people do not realize that they are paying more for clean air than they otherwise would, so they don't out-vote the small number of activists in the political market as they do in the private market. Thus, we get more clean air than people would want if they were free to negotiate for it.[12]

Finally, the environmentalists' last line of defense is the inevitability defense, just as the socialists ultimately resorted to the argument that socialism is an historical inevitability and therefore not subject to intellectual debate. Environmentalists bring up apocalyptic scenarios that demand coercive responses. Global warming and ozone depletion are examples; their potential costs are so high— the end of human civilization, more or less—that we can't wait for market solutions to evolve. Government must impose restrictions immediately at any cost to preserve life on the planet.

Science is showing that global warming and ozone depletion are no more inevitable than socialism, but, even so, environmentalists argue that we should act. Principle Nine of the vision statement of the President's Council on Sustainable Development asserts that "where public health may be adversely affected, or environmental damage may be serious or irreversible, prudent action is required even in the face of scientific uncertainty."[13] But given scientific uncertainty, how do you define "prudent action?" It must be determined politically, and we can expect a lot of imprudent, unneeded, and costly policies if politics determines the action to be taken.

Many are uneasy with the evolutionary market model. They feel that they are being asked to accept on faith the spontaneous and unpredictable forces of the market. They feel more comfortable with the proposition that we should, as a society, consciously plan our future in order to arrive at the desired ends. But such planning, we realize now, cannot achieve the desired ends. Of such planning Hayek once asked, "Is there a greater tragedy imaginable than that, in our endeavor consciously to shape our future in accordance with high ideals, we should in fact unwittingly produce the very opposite of what we have been striving for?"[14] A survey of US government policy in the last sixty years makes it painfully clear that the government's efforts have often aggravated the problems it was trying to solve. The track record of free societies and free institutions in satisfying human needs is far better than the track record of governments. Because of this, faith in the market is not blind, and relying on government, in light of its past performance, seems foolhardy.

Notes

1. Ludwig von Mises, *Human Action: A Treatise on Economics*, 3rd rev. ed. (Chicago: Henry Regnery Co., 1966), p. 700.

2. Friedrich A. Hayek, "The Use of Knowledge in Society," *American Economic Review* (September 1945), pp. 519-530.

3. Israel M. Kirzner, "Economic Planning and the Knowledge Problem," *Cato Journal* (Fall 1984), pp. 407-418.

4. For a comprehensive survey of the calculation debate, see Trygve J.B. Hoff, *Economic Calculation in the Socialist Society* (Indianapolis: Liberty Press, 1981).

5. Quoted from the letters to the editor in which there was exchange between Fred L. Smith, Jr., and Robert Stavins, "Let's Pretend Markets," *Policy Review* (Summer 1989), pp. 94-96.

6. See Michael Kellog, "After Environmentalism: Three Approaches to Managing Environmental Regulation," *Regulation*, no. 1 (1994), pp. 25-34.

7. Terry L. Anderson and P.J. Hill, "The Evolution of Property Rights: A Study of the American West," *Journal of Law and Economics*, vol. 12 (1975), pp. 163-179.

8. See Ronald H. Coase, "The Problem of Social Cost," *Journal of Law and Economics* (October 1960), pp. 1-44.

9. See Jonathan Adler, *Reforming Arizona's Air Pollution Policy*, (Phoenix: Goldwater Institute, 1993), pp. 9-10.

10. The private highway approach was suggested by Terry L. Anderson and Donald R. Leal in *Free Market Environmentalism* (Boulder, Colorado: Westview Press, 1991), p. 165.

11. Harold Demsetz, "Toward a Theory of Property Rights," *American Economic Review* (May 1967), pp. 347-360.

12. Of course other political factors may lead to less clean air than demanded. Because it is impossible for bureaucrats to know how much clean air people demand they may set the maximum level too high. This effectively creates a legally permissible amount of pollution, giving firms the right to pollute while depriving property owners of the ability to sue for damages.

13. President's Council on Sustainable Development, *Vision Statement and Principles of Sustainable Development*, Spring 1994.

14. Friedrich A. Hayek, *The Road to Serfdom* (Chicago: The University of Chicago Press, 1944), p. 5.

The Case Against Pollution Taxes

Fred L. Smith, Jr.

Mounting criticism of the conventional approach to environmental policy has stimulated reform efforts, particularly at the Environmental Protection Agency. Unfortunately, the emphasis has been on the methods used to advance politically determined environmental objectives, rather than on the direct problems of centralized political controls. Thus far, the environmental reform debate has focused on the relative merits of environmental taxes, tradable pollution permits, and other "market-oriented" policies, rather than the more fundamental issue of the inability of political institutions to develop rational environmental policy.

It is taken for granted that environmental goals will continue to be set politically. Now, however, "markets" will be harnessed to advance these political goals. Taxes, permits, and other "market mechanisms" will be used to improve the static efficiency of the system. This strategy represents the search for a Third Way between capitalism and socialism: market means to attain politically determined ends. Such a strategy was, of course, attempted in Eastern Europe and the former Soviet Union as "market socialism." Just as it failed in these instances, it will not meet with success in the realm of environmental policy.

Free Markets or "Market Socialism"?

Direct command-and-control regulations place little value on costs, provide little opportunity for efficient implementation,

---

Excerpted from *Europe, Energy and the Environment: The Case Against Carbon Taxes* (Washington, DC: Competitive Enterprise Institute, 1992).

and fail to encourage technical development. Many therefore call for augmenting government's regulatory powers with a broad range of "market mechanisms"—such as pollution taxes and tradable emission allowances or permits. Yet there is reason to question whether such changes improve environmental policy.

The evidence of similar experiments in the East suggest that we should not be optimistic. Socialist planners recognized that their economies were failing, and they recognized the advantages of market economies. Seeking to retain political determination of the economy's direction, they sought to introduce incentives and restraints to replicate the efficiencies of their Western counterparts. Yet their efforts still failed.

These programs failed because markets without property rights are a grand illusion. Without the system of decentralized control—private parties revealing their values through voluntary choices—the information to select meaningful environmental goals and the incentives to see that they are implemented are lacking. This process cannot be duplicated through administered prices, tax schemes, tradable rights, and the other efforts to manipulate market outcomes. Markets cannot be designed out of whole cloth, they evolve from the numerous interactions of a free people expressing their choices as to how their properties are to be used. That fact is not well understood even by many advocates of free market policies.

The core argument against market socialism, as forwarded by the likes of Ludwig von Mises and F.A. Hayek, is that central planners could not obtain the information and create the set of incentives needed to direct the modern economy. They simply never could possess the information needed to direct a modern economy. Moreover, even if such information could somehow be assembled, the planners would face the insurmountable task of inducing the population to obey the derived plan. It is important to remember that the efficiency gains of market systems occur not only in production, but in allocation as well. This means that markets are as effective at determining *what* is to be done as they are at determining *how* it should be accomplished.

The empirical case against this approach is evident in the failures of the communist experiments to introduce such market socialist reforms. Extremely bright people sought without success to create markets without private property, incentives from above, information by calculation. Their painful failures resulted both from the inability to acquire needed information and to create essential incentives, but also from the public choice problems to which all political decision arrangements are subject. The political process is prone to certain errors that make it extremely difficult for even well intentioned, capable, and honorable people to advance the public welfare. Using taxes and permits instead of command-and-control regulations does not address this concern. America's current tax regime is riddled with special interest provisions; an environmental tax code would be no different.

The real difficulties are not that a few selective uses of regulatory taxes or tradable government permits cannot have value, but rather that this is not what markets are all about. The world is well advised to minimize reliance on such gimmicks. Only a system of private property and private distribution creates the institutional framework within which individuals can directly decide how much bread and of what type they wish to purchase and produce. Without the information generated by actual exchange, we can not know beforehand what mix would actually benefit consumers, and we cannot replicate the efficiency and speed with which market arrangements modify that mix as tastes and costs change. Markets arise from the actions of people in their roles as both suppliers and consumers, and are not directed from above. In this sense, the market is best viewed as a discovery mechanism that is able to demonstrate the combined preferences of society for particular goods and services.

What we want, how to get it, and what costs it will impose are questions that remain unanswered in the environmental field. While many claim to know the answers, there is anything but a consensus. Differing groups have widely differing interests and expectations. Reconciling these diverse interests, motivating the search for better approaches, mapping out the unavoidable tradeoffs and assessing their relative values can only be achieved by creating real markets where both the means and the ends are determined through economic interaction. Our goal is not to achieve environmental objectives efficiently; it is to determine what environmental objectives are worthy of achievement in the first place.

None of this is to argue that taxes cannot affect behavior. Indeed, the United States has a long experience with various taxes used for various purposes. America's experience suggests that taxes will always be seen first and foremost as revenue sources—witness the use of tobacco taxes to fund various programs—and only second for other purposes. Where taxes are used to direct a desired policy outcome, it is typically to assist the elimination of a product from the marketplace altogether, such as leaded gasoline or chlorofluorocarbons. The empirical evidence argues against any reliance on taxes as a means to address the complex dynamic system of tradeoffs that are the nature of an efficient economy. Taxes and tradable permits may reduce the costs of such schemes, but they do not address the underlying policy question.

Nothing in the Environmental Protection Agency's experience with airshed bubbles or offset trading programs suggests any large advantages are likely to accrue from the use of such market mechanisms. Theoretical calculations of the gains of such tax-and-rights mechanisms normally presume that regulations will be implemented stupidly, while taxes will be implemented flawlessly. Neither presumption is accurate. High cost regulatory actions will be resisted more fiercely—making for delays, exemptions, variances, and other adjustments—all of which reduce regulatory costs. Tax mechanisms will be less specific than assumed—charging wide classes of disparate users similar fees—and will be subject to the same special variations of any government program. The differences between the two political intervention strategies are less than contemporary theory may suggest.

Markets depend upon stability and predictability. The illusion of market mechanisms is that such stability will be a key feature of the process. It will not. In the United States, government rule changes have played havoc with markets for pollution rights, and current law enshrines government's ability to continue to do so in the future. Government wants people to take these incentives seriously, to view pollution rights as "property," while still retaining the right to confiscate such rights at will, without review, without compensation. The history of such "markets" in the United States finds that they have been few, rarely utilized, often collapsing. Markets without property rights remain a fantasy of economic planners. They are not reforms that environmentalists should endorse if their goal is environmental progress.

What Is to Be Done?

The core of free market environmentalism lies in an emphasis on the institutional framework rather than the attainment of specific goals. Environmentalists should not seek to reduce emissions to some "acceptable" level but rather to empower the producers and recipients of this substance to reach a voluntary settlement. How else can we establish priorities as to which pollutants are most important to reduce and how and where to reduce them?

Does this mean that we should never use a politically created rights approach? No, but we should recognize that the right should be based on demonstrable environmental impacts rather than on the emissions of a particular substance. After all, it is the environmental impact—the trespass of pollution onto another's property—that should motivate the political intervention. A regime of tradable emission rights, such as sulfur oxides, or a tax on production inputs, such as the carbon-content of fuels, will have only an indirect relationship to the environmental goal pursued. This is particularly true when such measures are enacted at the national level. The same level of emissions will have starkly different impacts in different parts of the country. If a tax scheme is to have any pretense of "internalizing" the external impacts of pollution, regional differences must be taken into account. This means that there is no case for a national charge or rights system, but does leave the option of a local fee system, such as one that focuses on a given airshed.

When the framework seeks to approximate a market situation through some proxy, emissions are treated roughly the same irrespective of their impact. However, when the emphasis is on reducing pollution, that is, on the damage resulting from an emission rather than emission itself, then I am willing—albeit reluctantly—to consider pollution charges, tradable permits, and other market socialism approaches to environmental protection.

The general presumption that environmental problems require political solutions is wrong. It has led us to measures which threaten to cripple our economies, while doing little if anything to improve our ecologies. Measures which would take environmental policy seriously, and would seek ways of extending property rights to an ever-wider range of environmental resources, have thus far been rejected in favor of ever more intrusive political controls. The latest "reform" effort—a shift to taxes, permits, allowances, and the like—is only a marginal improvement. At a minimum, we should think carefully before imposing a pollution tax or other "faux market" regime.

❖❖❖❖❖ **Risk Issues**

The Risks of Risk Regulation

Jonathan H. Adler

Much of environmental regulation deals with risk—the risk of pesticides on food, the risk of groundwater contamination, the risk of industrial emissions, the risk of technological change, the risk of ecological disruption. Were Americans not concerned with these and other similar risks, much of the environmental regulation that is so hotly contested today would not exist.

The debate over environmental risk usually proceeds as follows: The media or an environmentalist lobbying group claims to have uncovered a new, insidious threat to human health and the environment. Almost immediately there is a call for the enactment of new regulations proscribing the use of some technology or process, and possibly even calling for the creation of a new government agency. A risk has been identified, and it must be eliminated. Through government regulation the world must be made a safer place. Opposing a risk regulation because the costs may outweigh the benefits is tantamount to placing a price tag on human life.

This is a typical story; it is how much environmental policy develops. Yet this story line, however familiar, is deceptive. It ignores the true nature of risk. Addressing risk always involves trade-offs; resources expended to reduce risk in one area cannot be used to reduce risk somewhere else as well. When regulations focus on smaller risks, at the expense of more threatening ones, they can do more harm than good. Regulations do not only impose economic costs, they can also harm human health and safety.

Portions adapted from "Deadly Fallout of Too Many Rules" and "Regulated...Out of this World" in the *Washington Times*, June 2 and 3, 1992.

There *are* environmental risks, and many of them deserve to be addressed. But it is wrong to think that merely because there are risks without government regulation that there are not risks created *by* government regulation. Indeed, there are risks on both sides of the regulatory equation: the risk of too little regulation, but also the risk of too much; the risk of technological development going too quickly, but also the risk of it going too slowly. When we only pay attention to one side of the trade-off between competing risks, we shortchange ourselves and encourage the formulation of bad environmental policy.

Consider the following example: The threat from asbestos seemed like a good reason to temporarily shut down schools in Peru, New York. After all, according to the media and the federal government, asbestos posed an unacceptable cancer risk when used for most applications. So the Peru Central School District closed several school buildings for a month, while junior and senior high school students went to classes 10 miles away in Plattsburgh, NY—classes that ended at 8:30 at night.[1]

By the time the asbestos removal was finished, the district had spent $3.5 million, more than 15 percent of its annual budget, on the removal of asbestos. Then the Environmental Protection Agency (EPA), the same agency that had enacted the asbestos ban, was forced to acknowledge that the threat of asbestos had been overestimated, and that the risks of improper removal were often greater than leaving it in place. What this means is that, if anything, asbestos regulations may have had an adverse impact on human health.

While more may have been spent in Peru than in other school districts, the story is much the same. Across the country, panicked parents and school administrators urged drastic action to protect their children from the threat of asbestos, a threat that had been greatly overstated. Nonetheless, defenders of the initial EPA policy will insist that such policies are justified as "insurance." After all, they ask, what are several thousand, several million, or even several billion dollars when you are seeking to protect human life? When put in terms of dollars versus deaths, there is no contest. Yet as the United States Fifth Circuit Court of Appeals stated in overturning several of the EPA's asbestos regulations, these rules can cost much more than money.[2]

According to the EPA's own estimate, these regulations would have prevented three premature deaths, over a period of thirteen years, at a cost of between $43 and $76 million per premature death averted. Investing that same amount of money on highway safety, early detection of breast cancer, or infant nutrition—or simply leaving that money in private hands for the purchase of life-enhancing goods and services—would have saved more lives. What is more, the EPA had even commissioned a study that indicated that asbestos substitutes might actually increase the number of fatalities. Yet despite this evidence, the agency enacted the bans.

Fortunately, the Fifth Circuit recognized a pernicious regulation when it saw one, and ruled against the EPA in *Corrosion Proof Fittings v. EPA*. "The EPA, in its zeal to ban asbestos, cannot overlook, with only cursory study, credible contentions that substitute products actually might increase fatalities," noted Judge Jerry Smith in his opinion for the court.[3]

This asbestos regulation is not an aberration; there remain a host of regulations that are responsible for increasing mortality. Compelling automakers to produce more fuel efficient vehicles forces individuals into lighter, less-safe cars, causing an estimated 2,000-4,000 deaths per year.[4] Withholding potentially life-saving drugs and treatments pending Food and Drug Administration (FDA) approval risks unnecessary deaths, particularly for those with life-threatening conditions.[5] Failure to chlorinate water for fear of minuscule cancer risks can cause thousands more deaths from outbreaks of cholera and other diseases.[6] There certainly may be small risks created by chlorinating our water; but these risks are nothing when compared to the risks posed by bacteria and waterborne disease should water supplies remain untreated.

Similarly, the government may be concerned with the risks posed by minute traces of pesticides that remain on foods. But insofar as pesticides increase food yields and enable more Americans to have balanced, healthy diets, the risks of fewer fruits and vegetables on America's dining room tables needs to be kept in mind, too. In 1996, the prestigious National Academy of Sciences confirmed that the risks of malnutrition are far greater than the risk of cancer from chemicals in the human diet.[7] Yet existing government regulations increase produce prices by limiting the ability of farmers to increase agricultural productivity.

State and local governments face the trade-offs between risks in another way. Local health officials are entrusted to reduce the health threats in their communities. When resources are expended in one area, they are not available to be expended in another. Thus, when federal policy forces a community to spend thousands of dollars to reduce one risk, other risks remain unaddressed. In this manner some federal policies actually frustrate efforts to reduce risk. In some communities significant risks, such as crime, cannot be adequately dealt with because thousands of dollars are required to be spent addressing hypothetical cancer risks instead. For example, for the cost of averting one premature death from the EPA's standard for benzene emissions, over three thousand police officers could be hired in a major city.[8] For the amount of money spent to avert one premature death under regulations governing coke ovens, over 470 lives could be saved through the purchase of lung cancer screenings. In economics this is known as an opportunity cost, and it is a real cost of environmental regulation.

A death is a death, whether caused by workplace exposure to airborne toxics or by less-effective, asbestos-free brake pads. When the policies of the federal government are directly responsible for the additional loss of life, those policies should be repealed.

Government agencies with a mission to make our lives "safer" should not be permitted to make us less safe.

While federal fuel economy standards and FDA drug lag are examples of "death by regulation," the federal government is increasingly causing death by regulation in an indirect manner as well. When advocates for increased regulation insist that the burdens of federal rules are more than compensated for by the benefits they provide, there is one item that they conveniently leave out of the equation: Burdensome regulations, in and of themselves, can increase mortality.

It is an indisputable fact that wealthier societies are healthier societies. Wealthier societies simply have more wealth to spend on things that improve the quality of life, from nutrition and health care to bicycle helmets and automobile child-safety seats. By the same token, societies and communities with fewer resources are less safe than they could otherwise be.[9]

According to James MacCrae, then acting-administrator of the Office of Information and Regulatory Affairs, "when national income falls, there is often a significant increase in mortality and a decline in health status."[10] For example, a 1984 study by Congress's Joint Economic Committee found that declines in real per capita income in the early 1970s led to a corresponding increase in total mortality, amounting to as many as 60,000 additional deaths.[11] Other studies estimate that every loss of between $3 million to $8 million to the economy will result in a premature death.[12] From a personal standpoint, losing one's job is one of the unhealthiest things that can happen due to the loss of a steady income. This means that when the economy sours, people die. The point is that regulations that depress national income—for whatever reason—create new risks from other less apparent sources.

The current economic burden of federal regulations is approximately $670 billion per year, according to the General Accounting Office—nearly $7000 per household.[13] Making the conservative assumption that there is a premature death for every $10 million lost to the economy, this would mean that federal regulations are responsible for as many as 64,700 premature deaths each year. It should also be no surprise that the vast majority of these deaths would occur in financially strapped communities where there is less institutional ability to compensate for economic losses. In a similar fashion, poorer countries are less able to mitigate the impact of economic declines than wealthier ones.

There certainly are environmental risks that merit attention, yet just as government regulation may alleviate risks, it may create them as well. Just because environmental risks exist does not mean that eliminating those risks with regulation will always produce a less risky world. Risks weigh against other risks, in everything we do. In this the environment is no different than anything else.

Notes

1. "School District in Chaos Over Asbestos Removal," *New York Times,* October 22, 1991.

2. *Corrosion Proof Fittings v. The Environmental Protection Agency,* 947 F.2d 1201 (5th Cir. 1991).

3. Ibid.

4. See Robert Crandall and John D. Graham, "The Effect of Fuel Economy Standards on Automobile Safety," *Journal of Law and Economics* (April 1989), pp. 110-115.

5. Sam Kazman, "Deadly Overcaution: FDA's Drug Approval Process," *Journal of Regulation and Social Costs* (September 1990), p. 48.

6. World Health Organization, "Cholera update, end of 1993," *Weekly Epidemiol. Rec.,* vol. 69 (1993), pp. 13-20.

7. National Research Council, *Carcinogens and Anticarcinogens in the Human Diet* (Washington, DC: National Academy Press, 1996), pp. 303-312.

8. John C. Shanahan and Adam Thierer, "Can We Save Even More Lives? Understanding the 'Opportunity Costs' of Regulation," Heritage Foundation *F.Y.I.,* no. 11, February 28, 1994.

9. Aaron Wildavsky, *Searching for Safety* (New Brunswick, New Jersey: Transaction Books, 1988).

10. James B. Macrae, Jr., Statement before the Senate Committee on Governmental Affairs, March 19, 1992.

11. US Congress, Joint Economic Committee, "Estimating the Effects of Economic Change on National Health and Social Well-Being," J842-38 (Washington, DC: Government Printing Office, 1984).

12. See, for example, Ralph Keeney, "Mortality Risks Induced by Economic Expenditures," *Risk Analysis*, vol. 10, no. 1 (1990), pp. 147-159.

13. Thomas D. Hopkins, "Prepared Statement of Thomas D. Hopkins: Rochester Institute of Technology, Rochester, New York Before The House Government Reform and Oversight Committee, National Economic Growth, Natural Resources and Regulatory Affairs Subcommittee," May 16, 1996.

Privatizing Risk

Fred L. Smith, Jr.

Risk has always been with us, and it always will be. Dealing with it requires good judgment and a sense of balance; it involves degrees of uncertainty and, invariably, an element of danger. Dealing with risk politically is quite another matter.

There is widespread agreement that the Environmental Protection Agency's (EPA) risk-management policies have gone astray. Some of the EPA's failures—clean fuel regulations that benefit ethanol producers; a Superfund program that has created a vast pork barrel—conform to the traditional political pattern of favoring special interests under the guise of serving the public interest. Other failures fall in the category of misguided risk selection: The Clean Water Act requires enormous investments to abate so-called pollution that has no discernible effect on water quality, while Superfund mandates extravagantly expensive "permanent" treatment options, with the result that hundreds of sites remain entirely untreated.

The challenge to improve on this performance is evident and urgent. According to the EPA, by 1992 America invested well in excess of $100 billion per year in environmental protection. We should seek to ensure that these vast resources are directed to abate genuine risks and that they are used as efficiently as possible.

However, inefficiency and misguided risk selection may not be the EPA's most serious failures. As disappointing as these out-

---

A longer version of this essay originally appeared as "Environmental Policy at the Crossroads" in *Environmental Politics: Public Costs, Private Rewards*, Michael S. Greve and Fred L. Smith, Jr., eds. (New York: Praeger, 1992).

comes are, they are not altogether surprising in light of our experience with grand social schemes in general. When it comes to inefficiency and misdirection of resources, there is no great difference in principle between the war on poverty and the war on environmental risk. Rather, the distinctive, and most fateful, consequence of environmental regulation has been a complete transformation of public expectations regarding risk. We expect insurers to mitigate the effects of unfortunate events, not to prevent their occurrence, and we expect doctors to cure diseases (most of them, anyway), not to make us immortal. Not so with governmental risk managers: We have come to expect that the EPA—and, for that matter, the Food and Drug Administration (FDA) and other "social" regulatory agencies—will *eliminate* risk. This expectation is as much the *result* of modern environmental risk management as it is its source. Statutes such as Superfund, the Clean Air Act, and the Clean Water Act incorporate binding commitments to zero risk and an absolutely clean environment.

By promising the impossible, though, government sets itself up for failure. The result is an environmental version of Gresham's law: Utopian but horribly flawed regulatory schemes drive out more realistic, imperfect, but acceptable, policies. Having been promised, and having come to expect, a totally clean environment, the public is not readily persuaded that it must make do with less. The utopian pretensions of environmental programs, and the public misperceptions induced by those pretensions, pose a most serious obstacle to environmental policy reform.

One may be tempted to conclude that the combination of government-sponsored ignorance and entrenched interests may doom any prospect for more sober, realistic, and effective environmental risk management. However, growing disenchantment with current "command and control" policies may create a basis for reform. Moreover, one can at least hope that the dynamics of inflated public expectations will, in the long run, do more to undermine than to sustain the demand for comprehensive regulatory schemes. Government cannot possibly succeed in attaining the unattainable, and as the real and perceived failures multiply, we may eventually begin to address the question of what has gone wrong with the seriousness it deserves.

Broadly speaking, the reforms now under discussion fall into two categories. One of these comprises managerial reforms such as an emphasis on sound science, improved risk assessment procedures, and better interagency cooperation. As I will argue below, such reforms can remedy the more fundamental flaws of environmental regulation only to a limited extent and only if they change or at least counteract the political and institutional incentives that currently produce inefficient regulation and biased risk selection. The second category of reforms contains "incentive-based" or "market-based" regulatory tools, such as emission fees and tradable emission permits. Such devices represent a welcome departure from the exclusive reliance on command-and-control regulation, and some of them might result in more efficient, less wasteful environmental regulation, which is a worthy goal. However, as I shall argue, incentive-based environmental regulation is no panacea and may even exacerbate some of the defects of command-and-control regulation. The fundamental problem of market-based regulation is that risks would continue to be selected and regulated on political grounds, with all the attendant opportunities for special interest mischief, political abuse, and false promises.

For this reason, the case for *private* environmental risk management deserves consideration. Reconsideration would be the more accurate term: Until not long ago, risk management was considered predominantly a private responsibility. Most significant resources at risk were privately owned, and their owners protected them—in the extreme case, through use of the courts—against trespass, theft, and other risks. Individuals negotiated on risk matters, typically through contractual agreements.

Private parties paid to shift risks to private insurance firms; private rating services provided information about the nature and level of risk in countless fields.

Today, however, private risk management devices are frequently dismissed as impractical or as objectionable for other reasons, at least in the environmental context, and such dismissals are usually accepted as soon as they are voiced. America seems to have fallen in love with political risk management. How did this romance start?

Sources of Political Risk Management

The beliefs that government must manage and even eliminate environmental risk, and that only government can do so, can be traced to two sources. First, and most obviously, America has become obsessed with risk. Americans are among the healthiest, wealthiest people in history. And yet, we worry.

This is not a paradox: The taste of zero risk is one in which only the richest and most advanced societies can indulge. Indeed, our growing wealth and health are partially responsible for the growing discontent over the remaining residual risks we face: Having attained much, we want it all. We want no changes that entail risks. We are no longer content to take the bitter uncertainty with the sweet progress; instead, we insist on having the sweet only and rely on the government to protect us in advance from the bitter.

However, as Aaron Wildavsky has shown, the effort to "have it all" is paradoxical and futile.[1] It is paradoxical because societies become safer only by replacing the old with the new. Familiar products give way to newer ones that turn out to be safer (commercially canned foods instead of home canning) and less polluting (electric heating instead of wood stoves). This is itself a risky course; it involves reliance on such engines of change as science and technology, and it requires us to overcome our fears of the unknown. At the same time, we underestimate the extent to which scientific progress and increased economic wealth have made us safer and healthier; nostalgia has a way of concealing the unpleasant aspects of the past. When we think of travel in the pre-automotive era, we tend to forget the huge disposal problems created by horse wastes and carcasses. When we think of man's effect on nature, we forget nature's often cataclysmic effects, and we underestimate the extent to which material progress has enabled us to temper those effects.[2]

The effort to have it all is futile, because attempts to eliminate risk are both tremendously expensive and, quite often, self-defeating in unexpected ways. "Playing it safe, doing nothing, means reducing possible opportunities to benefit from chances taken, and can hurt people."[3] Prometheus, the god of technology, brought fire—a fearful and very risky new technology. However, these new risks—of burns and asphyxiation, for instance—produced far fewer casualties than had the earlier risks of exposure to the elements, vulnerability to wild animals, and starvation. Thus, the introduction of fire compares favorably to the contemporary approval process of pharmaceutical drugs, which requires manufacturers to spend years of expensive research and studies to prove a new drug will be "safe and effective." The possibility that the new drug, though dangerous, might be less dangerous than the remedies now extant—which may be none at all—receives little consideration. The resulting "drug lag" has made the United States a far more dangerous place.[4]

Once society demands the elimination of risk, government gains a vast advantage over private risk management. Only government would even purport to pursue the utopian goal of eliminating risk; only government has the power and the resources to make such a claim remotely credible. Only the political process makes it possible to compensate losers—with no regard for their own co-responsibility—by raising revenues from less visible and less powerful sources. Only politicians promise "free" health care, "zero" pollution, and "zero" risk.

The desire for zero risk dovetails with a general distrust of markets and corporations. The underlying notion is that the profit motive encourages businesses to cut corners and sacrifice safety and the environment for profits. This notion either presupposes that neither consumers nor their "middlemen" (such as insurers, rating agencies, or purchasers somewhere along a product's distribution chain) can adequately assess the risks of a product or service; or else it presupposes that most private actors are "onetime players" who are indifferent to the prospect of obtaining repeat business.[5] One cannot otherwise explain how the knowing endangerment of one's customers could be a profit-maximizing strategy.

Of course, private parties make mistakes. Pipes leak, containment dikes give way, and control or treatment technologies fail unexpectedly. Private systems are not immune from sabotage or error, either. For those predisposed to distrust markets, oil spills and drug poisonings signify the inevitable and catastrophic consequences of environmental failures in free and unregulated markets. It appears, therefore, individuals cannot be trusted to concern themselves adequately with the risks created by their activities.

However, *all* private transactions pose a risk of market failure in the (nontechnical) sense that they may produce, individually or in the aggregate, social results that are widely considered undesirable. Private transactions may perpetuate social inequality; competition destroys once-flourishing businesses. Still, we have, on the whole, become rather skeptical of attempts to remedy such ills by replacing private arrangements with grandiose regulatory schemes. It is only when it comes to the protection of health, safety, and the environment that alleged market failures are considered irrefutable evidence of the need for drastic government intervention. Government regulation seems singularly compelling in the environmental area.

In part, this is the case because many private activities do produce environmental *externalities*—that is, costs that are not reflected in the price of a product or service. Factories and cars do pollute the air, and as long as the air they use is "free," there will be too much air pollution.

Appealing as the market failure argument may seem, though, it is too facile. The fact that markets are imperfect does not, in itself, demonstrate the superiority of political strategies; rather, it calls for a balanced comparison of the respective ability of private and political institutions to advance the public good.

More fundamentally, the market failure argument proves far too much. If the mere existence of externalities were a sufficient basis for government control, political intervention would be appropriate in virtually every economic decision: Practically every private transaction has *some* effect on outside parties or resources. In the end, externalities are limited solely by our ability to detect and measure them.

This threat of boundless externalities, every one of them requiring political intervention, is not imaginary. Until not so long ago, the EPA regulated only a handful of bulk pollutants emitted from a few major sources—for example, large factories belching smoke and urban sewage flowing untreated into the sea. Now, environmental statutes mandate the control of substances at concentration levels that could not even be detected a decade ago. The EPA is rapidly gaining central planning authority over the entire US economy. Six years ago, Richard B. Stewart, a law professor and member of the Board of the Environmental Defense Fund who, under the Bush Administration, became Assistant Attorney General for Environmental and Natural Resources, observed that environmental regulations and statutes had "created an elaborate system of Soviet-style centralized planning for the production of a clean environment."[6] Stewart's observation predates the 1986 Superfund Amendments, the 1987 Amendments to the Clean Water Act, the 1990 Clean Air Act Amendments, and various other enactments that vastly expanded the existing centralized planning schemes. In contrast to the Soviets, who at least had the wisdom to declare victory with the failure of each five-year plan, we seem to use defeat as a springboard for intensified folly.

Unless we want to march mindlessly down the road mapped out by the market failure paradigm, we must begin to take the task of environmental reform seriously. In this essay I will argue that managerial and regulatory reforms may play a useful role in this endeavor. In the end, however, meaningful reform depends on our ability to recognize that the failures of environmental regulation are rooted not in markets but in their *absence*.

Better Management or Institutional Reform?

The increasingly widespread recognition of the failures and follies of environmental policy has prompted increasingly urgent calls for reforms of the EPA's decision-making processes. Once confined to a narrow circle of economists, the chorus for reform has been joined by political scientists, policy analysts, and, recently, by the EPA itself.[7] The reform agenda encompasses proposals such as improved scientific and risk assessment procedures, increased public participation in the agency's decision-making process, and government-sponsored public education on risk and environmental matters.

While these and other proposals merit consideration, they are ultimately unlikely to address the serious failures of environmental regulation. Those failures do not occur randomly or, for that matter, as a result of bad management (although this may occasionally be the case). Rather, they stem from deep-rooted institutional and political incentives that systematically bias the EPA's decisions. Better science and risk assessment procedures, public participation, and civic education, in and of themselves, do little to counteract these biases, and may exacerbate them.

Science will not automatically inform the policy debate. Scientific findings reach decision-makers only through the distorting prism of political power, and they are used in a political context. The examples of the political use and abuse of science are legion. A recent and particularly dramatic instance is the fate of the National Acid Precipitation Assessment Project (NAPAP), a massive 10-year study of the effects of acid rain.[8] The study, which was released in early 1990, failed to confirm earlier suggestions that acid rain might be creating major damage to lakes and forests throughout America. By that stage the Bush administration and congressional leaders had already committed themselves to an extravagantly expensive acid rain program. The NAPAP study was shelved by the EPA and never received a full hearing in Congress. It is safe to say that the NAPAP study would have received quite a different treatment if it had confirmed the worst fears about acid rain and, thus, lent credibility to the legislation then under consideration. In short, the extent to which science informs policy depends largely on its political acceptability and usefulness.

Enhanced public participation, also on the reform agenda, is similarly incapable of counteracting the incentives that bias political risk management. Almost invariably, participation is not "public" but highly selective. For the public, the costs of obtaining sufficient information and setting aside sufficient time to participate in a meaningful way are prohibitive. The likely participants are either business interests, who can easily bear the cost of the attorneys and lobbyists that the regulation game entails, or leaders and attorneys of ideological interest groups, who systematically favor comprehensive government intervention and whose views have consistently been found to be highly unrepresentative even of the membership of those groups, never mind the public at large.[9] In effect, public participation shifts power from the uninvolved majority to intensely concerned interests, and it increases the likelihood of political over private resolution of environmental issues. As a result, public participation has a tendency to exacerbate an already existing bias against the new and for the old; for entrenched interests and against the as-yet unidentified producers and consumers of improved products.

This is also the case with civic education, a proposal that has been advanced by both policy analysts and by the EPA. It is unquestionably true that the public is often inadequately informed or positively misinformed about the nature of environmental risk. (This very essay calls for a radical revision of the way in which we as a society think about risk—a civic education project of monumental proportions.) However, civic education is an undertaking fraught with perils, especially when it is done by government.

In a very real sense, ignorance may not only be bliss but may also be rational: It serves as a filter that tends to screen out remote and exotic risks, thus leading individuals to occupy themselves with more substantial ones. It may seem desirable that individuals be made aware of *all* environmental dangers, including those posed by minute trace amounts of carcinogens. Realistically, though, people have no way of comparing these risks to anything in the real world; they become subject to information overload and scare campaigns.

To be sure, scare campaigns would be staged with or without government-sponsored civic education, and there might be a real role for the EPA in countering shrill but false fire alarms and calling attention to genuine risks. However, experience shows that we cannot trust government to correct public misperceptions. The line between education and propaganda is not always very clear, and it is crossed with particular ease when the issues are highly uncertain, as they typically are in the environmental context, and when a political agency has an incentive to emphasize risks that fall within its jurisdiction, as does the EPA. As Marc K. Landy has shown, the enactment of Superfund was accompanied by an intense EPA public relations campaign aimed at persuading the public that the agency's public health programs were necessary to abate immediate and mortal risks.[10] The campaign was plainly motivated by a device to build political support for an expansion of the agency's mandate and budget.

The purpose of these admittedly sketchy deliberations is not so much to question the usefulness of better science, public participation, and civic education but, rather, to show that the usefulness of these policies and practices depends on the political and institutional context within which they are utilized. It is that *context*, which produces biased and misguided decisions, that needs reform. While this is not the place to outline a master plan for reform, we can state the general principle any reform should satisfy, and provide a few examples of promising proposals.

The general principle is to introduce reforms that simulate and institutionalize the competing and conflicting considerations that should inform the management of environmental risk. Currently, some of these considerations enter into the EPA's decisions only in a highly distorted form; others are ignored altogether. Decisions are made centrally and far away from those who incur their costs and benefits, thus practically ensuring they will be influenced more by considerations of regulatory feasibility—and by national lobbies—than by the concerns of those who have to live with the results. The costs of regulation enter the decision-making process largely in a conceptual form: The agency may consider costs, but it does not bear them. Moreover, the EPA's mandate to preserve the environment and to protect the public naturally incline it toward regulation and against technological innovation, as does the fact that the potential beneficiaries of products and processes that are yet to be introduced and invented are unrepresented in the decision-making process. Institutional and procedural reforms should counteract these and other incentives that create a regulatory fantasy land.

To an extent, such reforms can be accomplished within the existing regulatory structure. The EPA has, on occasion, experimented with regional, decentralized risk management and encouraged participation by those directly affected by regulatory decisions. For example, the EPA effectively suspended the imposition of a clean air technology standard that would have shut down a copper smelter in Tacoma, Washington, and held local meetings with the goal of having local residents determine the appropriate level of pollution control and to make the trade-off between jobs and clean air. (The smelter closed for unrelated reasons before the experiment was concluded.)

The Superfund reform scheme proposed by Marc K. Landy and Mary Hague is a variation on this theme of decentralization and greater local control.[11] Their proposal would allocate a fixed sum to each state for Superfund cleanup. Each state would then face the decisions now made by the EPA, such as the selection of sites and cleanup options. This proposal would bring the decision closer to those concerned; it has the added and considerable advantage of introducing real-world concerns of economic scarcity and of destroying the illusion that toxic site cleanup is free. As Landy and Hague show, it is this illusion—which is carefully nurtured by Superfund's beneficiaries and by their congressional patrons—that has made Superfund an ineffective and wasteful program.

In order to counter the EPA's institutional and political bias against innovation, jurisdiction over industries and technologies that have not yet clearly been assigned to an agency (for example, biotechnology) should be conferred on agencies having both a regulatory and promotional policy role, or at least should be designed to strengthen the role of promotional agencies in the interagency regulatory review. Biotechnology regulation would be managed much better by the US Department of Agriculture than by the EPA or, for that matter, the FDA. Since the Agriculture Department is charged both with protecting food safety *and* with improving agricultural productivity, it is far more likely to weigh the benefits of biotechnology as well as its potential risks than is the EPA, which has no promotional role.

This jurisdictional solution is not a serious option with respect to regulatory responsibilities that have already been clearly established; the EPA is highly unlikely to relinquish its powers.

Accordingly, we should consider establishing an Office of the Technology Advocate—a sort of devil's advocate agency which would be charged with making the most compelling case possible *against* regulatory impositions in the environmental risk area.[12] The Technology Advocate's Office would receive a fixed percentage of the EPA's budge, which would protect the office against political pressures, and it would obtain access to all agency data. In addition, the office might be permitted to pocket, for its own operations, some percentage of the projected cost savings of its activities. The office would provide an access point for—and might actually seek to mobilize—constituencies that are currently frozen out of the regulatory process or that are unlikely to participate but likely to bear the costs of regulation, such as small businesses, nonunionized workers, and economically disadvantaged groups that suffer disproportionately from particular regulations.

As part of its duties, the office might conduct a "postregulatory approval audit," estimating the public health and economic costs accrued to the delay of approval for such products as pesticides and other agricultural products. Sam Kazman has proposed such an audit for the FDA which, like the EPA, is highly biased against the risks of innovation and largely indifferent to the risks of stagnation and delay. Kazman's proposal would have the FDA (or possibly a third party) prepare detailed estimates of the public health costs of the "drug lag"—that is, delays in the drug approval process.[13] A requirement for public, official acknowledgments of risks that are now largely ignored in the regulatory process would eventually encourage a more balanced decision-making process. It would begin to stimulate, albeit crudely, real life for agency decision-makers.

Market-Based Regulation

As the inefficiencies of command-and-control regulation and centralized ecological planning have become more evident, proposals have proliferated to replace planning with more flexible, market-based approaches, such as pollution taxes and tradable emission rights.[14] Such schemes seek to replicate the efficiency of normal markets by introducing pollution costs as a factor in private investment and product decisions. Proponents see such devices as means of internalizing the external costs of pollution and, thus, of encouraging more ecologically-sensitive behavior.

In principle, such market-based schemes do offer several advantages. They reduce the regulators' need for information and technical expertise. Regulators need to determine only the overall price or quantity of pollution; the pollution sources themselves then decide which firms would clean up to what degree. Since these sources know more about their respective cost structures and technology options, they are more likely to identify least-cost compliance methods. Market-based schemes also offer greater flexibility; productive (though polluting) activities are not banned outright, but instead can continue where they are most valuable. Moreover, in contrast to mandated technology approaches, market-based schemes improve the visibility of pollution control costs, which may encourage greater attention to the costs and benefits of each particular pollution control program or, at least, reduce the tendency to view environmental protection as a "free" good. Finally, if the charges or financial burdens of emission rights schemes are imposed directly on polluters and in proportion to their actual pollution output, they will tend to produce long-term improvements in the availability and selection of pollution-reducing technologies and operating policies.

Still, market-based schemes have serious flaws, which stem from the fact that all such schemes embody the fundamental assumption that the socially desirable level of pollution must be determined politically.[15] Even so-called pollution rights are *not* private property but solely a function of politically predetermined goals. Thus, the initial allocation of pollution entitlements or taxation levels will be subject to the very same political influences and systemic biases that now distort government decisions on risk. This is true, for instance, of the acid rain "emission-trading" program in the 1990 Clean Air Act Amendments, which has been widely hailed as an efficient and innovative program.[16] Surely the real tax code—in many ways, a compendium of special interest provisions—inspires no confidence that a pollution tax code would be designed in accordance with objective environmental criteria as opposed to being determined by political clout. Moreover, the predetermined goals and, hence, the "rights" remain subject to political intervention and revision. Some groups will always find current standards too permissive, and firms may find themselves stripped of legitimately acquired emission rights. The desire to maximize revenue may soon drive out attempts to impose financial burdens in proportion to the actual externalities produced by each polluter. Highway user fees have taken this route: Trucks with very heavy axle loadings pay far less than warranted by the road damage they cause, while cars driving during off-peak hours are heavily overcharged.

Further, while incentive-based schemes may make regulation more efficient in a technical sense, they may also make it *easier*. For example, the EPA and Congress shun plant closures; for that reason, they seek to impose the toughest requirements on solvent firms while going easy on firms facing economic difficulties. Such strategies—which bear no relation to the actual amount of pollution output but take "from each according to their ability"—are difficult to implement through technology-based standards (although the EPA has managed to accomplish the feat); they become easier via taxing schemes, which can be set at a level just low enough to persuade the firm to continue operations.[17]

Finally, and most seriously, taxes and emission rights emphasize means rather than ends. However, as noted earlier, the EPA's primary problem is its inability to set well-defined, environmentally sound priorities. Focussing on implementation, rather than goals, would thus address the wrong first question.

In the end, market-based regulatory schemes are not genuine markets but market knockoffs. They are the ecological equivalent of the Eastern European experiments with market socialism during the 1970s and 1980s, which also sought to attain politically determined objectives by means of incentives and without establishing private property rights. The markets that resulted from these experiments were mere caricatures of real markets. Prices were artificial constructs and failed to provide the information and incentives needed to equilibrate supply and demand. Market socialism failed to invigorate innovation and productivity; eventually, it proved only marginally more efficient than Soviet-style command economies.

Command-and-control regulation is an attempt to produce environmental goods the way the Soviet Union produced (or failed to produce) shoes. Market-based environmental regulation is an effort to produce environmental goods in the way in which Hungary produced shoes two decades ago. This is a small step forward. We can, however, do better: Just as some Eastern European countries are moving aggressively to privatize their economies, we can begin to reacquaint ourselves with producing environmental goods through property rights and private, voluntary arrangements.

Private Risk Management

We have become so used to the idea that the socially acceptable levels of environmental risk and pollution must be determined politically that we find it hard to even contemplate the alternative. The very concept of "free market environmentalism" seems oxymoronic.

However, we have this reaction only when it come to *environmental* risk. We do not normally believe that the government should determine and enforce socially acceptable levels of private

activities—even if these activities create substantial risks and negative externalities for third parties.[18] The most instructive example is
economic competition, which entails the risk, and often the reality,
of business failures, job losses, and, sometimes, the ruin of entire
cities or regions. It is true, of course, that the political landscape is
littered with laws and regulations aimed at sheltering particular firms
and economic sectors against the forces of competition, and that the
antitrust laws are intended to guard against unusual breakdowns in
the competitive process. But such protectionist measures and government guarantees have lost much of their intellectual respectability,
as well as a large measure of public support; we have come to understand that they help special interests but hurt the public at large.
Nobody would maintain that the United States government should,
as a general matter and for reasons of public welfare, determine and
enforce a socially acceptable level of competition.

There are two reasons we generally tolerate the externalities
of competition. First, we understand that economic competition is
a process of creative destruction, and that we cannot prevent the
externality of destruction without losing the benefits of creativity
and innovation. Second, and perhaps more important, we understand that the alternative to centralized political management is not
anarchy; it is private, decentralized risk management. We all seek
to regulate our behavior—to anticipate the consequences of our
actions and to act accordingly. In fact,

> [centralized political] planning owes its popularity
> largely to the fact that everybody desires, of course,
> that we should handle our common problems as ra-
> tionally as possible and that, in so doing we should
> use as much foresight as we can command. In this
> sense, everybody who is not a complete fatalist is a
> planner, every political act is (or ought to be) an act
> of planning, and there can be differences only between

good and bad, between wise and foresighted and foolish and shortsighted planning....But it is not in this
sense that our enthusiasts for a planned society now
employ this term....The dispute between the modern
planners and their opponents is, therefore, *not* a dispute on whether we ought to choose intelligently
between the various possible organizations of society; it is not a dispute on whether we ought to employ
foresight and systematic thinking in planning our common affairs. It is a dispute about what is the best way
of so doing.[19]

The question, in other words, is not whether risks should be managed, but who should manage them.

Private and political risk managers face many of the same
problems: They must review the data, assess the level and nature of
the risks involved, and determine the appropriate response. The
case for *private* risk management rests on the proposition that the
information on which such decisions should be based is far too dispersed and fragmentary to permit central planning. The political
authority must make decisions for millions of individuals; since the
"optimal" level of risk is largely a function of private, idiosyncratic
preferences, the political risk manager would have to aggregate those
preferences and, ideally, weigh them in some proportion to their
intensity and their proximity to any given risk—a task for which
even the wisest official is thoroughly ill-equipped. Moreover, even
if he could somehow achieve this incredible feat, the political risk
manager would still face the even more daunting task of motivating
millions of people to act in accordance with his decrees.

One might argue that the accurate aggregation of private preferences is too demanding a standard to require of the political
decision-maker. The point, though, is that *private risk management
allows us to approximate that standard*: Myriads of voluntary

transactions register private risk preferences and tolerances far more accurately than even the most informed and open political process.

Consider the risks associated with transporting waste materials across private property. Under a private system, the shipper would require the approval of the property owner to transit the property and would likely agree to pay a fee for that privilege. The parties would reach an agreement on the procedures to be followed in the event of an accident. Both would seek ways to shift their residual risks, and private insurance firms would evolve to meet that demand. Specialized risk managers might be trained by one or all the parties to the transaction. The exact agreements would differ depending on the perceived riskiness of the transportation activity, the nature of the cargo, the extent to which the property would be harmed in the event of an accident, the property owner's attitude toward risk, and other considerations. Private arrangements, in other words, would take full account of the parties' concerns (but *only* the parties' concern: Third parties might comment on private arrangements, but they would have no power to modify or influence them).

Although, of course, some parties will "get it wrong" and underestimate the risks involved in such a transaction, one can expect the private actor to generally outperform the political actor on a one-to-one basis. However, the proper comparison is not between the political risk manager and the average private actor but between the politician and the one marginal private actor who, among millions of others, gets it right: His decision will soon dominate the market.

A political risk management regime, on the other hand, will produce outcomes different from those that would be agreed on by private parties; that, indeed, is the purpose of the exercise. Negotiations of transit rights over politically-controlled rights-of-way will involve public hearings which, as we have seen, selectively empower groups with an intense economic or ideological stake in the decision. Established economic firms may well use the occasion to restrict competition; for example, barge operators will lobby for high transit fees for truckers and railroads so as to raise their rivals' costs. Environmental groups, none of them with a genuine interest in the controversy other than an ideological one, may oppose transit rights on any conditions. In the end, the outcome may reflect *no one's* risk preferences.

Finally, private risk managers are far more likely than political institutions to consider risks in an unbiased fashion. Risks are ubiquitous; any decision will increase some risks and reduce others. The question is whether any given decision will raise or lower overall risk. Consider the question of whether a new technological process or product should be approved: The risks of innovation are heavily weighed by both private and political agencies. Change is dangerous, and no private or political actor wishes to assume the liabilities associated with approving a harmful innovation. On the other hand, stagnation and doing nothing are also dangerous. If only for competitive reasons, a private firm will take the risk of stagnation seriously. Few political risk managers, in contrast, experience any pain by delaying or even blocking change. The victims of inaction are statistical artifacts of a healthier and safer world that might have been; rarely do they weigh significantly in the political process.

Market Failures Considered

Admittedly, the preceding section was based on somewhat idealized assumptions. Notably, it did not deal with instances in which private parties can impose external costs on society and avoid paying.

While such situations are common, they are not caused by the existence of markets but by their *absence*. Market failures might, therefore, best be addressed by extending market arrangements to the widest possible array of environmental resources. As the economist Ludwig von Mises stated:

It is true that where a considerable part of the costs incurred are external costs from the point of view of the acting individuals or firms, the economic calculation established by them is manifestly defective and their results deceptive. But this is not the outcome of alleged deficiencies inherent in the system of private ownership of the means of production. It is on the contrary a consequence of loopholes left in the system. It could be removed by a reform of the laws concerning liability for damages inflicted and by rescinding the institutional barriers preventing the full operation of private ownership.[20]

Rather than viewing the world in terms of market failure, we should view the problem of externalities as a *failure to permit markets* and create markets where they do not yet—or no longer—exist. As a practical matter, we may wish to begin by experimenting with private risk-management solutions in limited areas where the case for them seems especially compelling. Although the project of creating markets seems similar to market-based regulation, the differences are substantial—and all-important: A genuine market based on property rights privatizes not only the *how* of risk control but also the *what* and the *how much*.

A comparison with the ordinary risk of trespass illustrates the significance of this difference. We do not have a Federal Bureau of Trespass charged with defining the socially optimal level of trespass (certainly not one charged with *eliminating* trespass). The decision as to whether a trespass has occurred is left to private property owners, who also determine whether the benefits of punishing any given incident of trespass are worth the costs. Casual transit is likely to be ignored by all but the misanthrope, as will the occasional windblown litter and the smoke from the neighbor's fireplace; more serious events will trigger more serious responses. Pollution

Fred L. Smith, Jr.

is no different in principle. (In fact, many landmark legal cases that defined the law of tort and trespass involved pollution.)

It is often objected that private arrangements are infeasible for practical and technical reasons. Emissions may be too small to constitute trespass, but, in the aggregate, they may do a lot of harm. Moreover, private property requires proof of trespass, and in many cases, the nature of the pollutant and the distances involved make such proofs difficult.

These problems are real, but they require closer analysis. To begin with, tossing them into the political sector does not make them any less difficult: it simply changes the range of possible solutions—and possible error. Since the optimal level of pollution is not *no* pollution, it is possible to err in both directions. Under a private regime, proof problems and the like will sometimes cause a failure to abate pollution. The political manager, in contrast, can limit pollution even without proof of damage (although, as we have noted, politically preferred polluters may still escape controls). But this strength of government is also a great danger: In the absence of identifiable harm to someone or something in particular, the costs and benefits of risk control become highly conjectural. Moreover, precisely *because* no showing of harm is required to justify regulatory intervention, the purpose of pollution control is eventually disconnected from *any* harm; the productive activity that generates externalities itself becomes the harm. This, precisely, is the logic of the Clean Air and the Clean Water Acts.

There is a second, equally fundamental point. The facile comparison between the private and the political ignores the innovative capacity of the market and the stifling nature of government risk management. The private market's response to enforcement problems is not paralysis; it is innovation. The invention of fencing technologies—such as the development of barbed wire that permitted the fencing of vast areas in the West—is one common response to the problems of enforcing property rights, as was the earlier creation of cooperative joint-venture arrangements to protect grazing lands from roaming cattle. But innovation *depends* on property rights. A world without private property might never, or only belatedly, have developed locks, burglar alarms, fingerprinting, and other tools to protect property. Moreover, the great variety in people's sensitivities to pollution and other externalities suggests that a range of innovative solutions will be explored far in advance of the dramatic events that are typically needed to trigger political responses.

The fact that these technologies *were* developed shows that markets are not rigid, frozen arrangements unable to address emerging concerns. Private environmental risk management would create demand for monitoring and chemical fingerprinting, which could identify the culprits responsible for oil spills and toxic dumping. Environmental regulators, in contrast, have no incentive to promote or use such technologies and may even view them as a threat to their authority.

One can concede that there are genuinely difficult issues for which private, voluntary solutions are difficult to imagine; global warming and ozone depletion come to mind. But one must suspect that these problems rank so high on the political agendas precisely *because* they seem to illustrate the failures of the markets, *because* they seem to defy private solution and the failures of markets, and *because* they seem to require comprehensive government interventions. In any event, it is one thing to observe that there are difficult and seemingly intractable environmental problems; it is quite a different thing to conceptualize all environmental issues from the perspective of those problems or to presume that a political approach will easily overcome these difficulties. The former is a useful observation; the latter, a dangerous mistake that forecloses innovative and effective private risk-management options even where they are feasible and sorely needed.

Conclusion

A politically owned resource is a resource at risk, and a politically managed risk is a risk that is on the verge of unmanageability. These two precepts do much to explain the current state of EPA regulation.

They do not explain everything. The EPA suffers from the usual panoply of bureaucratic failures; an urge to be seen as "doing something," a hankering for the dramatic, an inability to reject trendy pseudo-crises, and a disregard for the costs that it imposes on private parties. But no other agency shares the EPA's ability to create and chase indeterminate and indeterminable hazards. No other agency operates with such a total lack, not only of performance criteria, but of even the *prospect* of performance criteria.

A move toward private ownership would mean little unless such ownership encompassed the rights to use and transfer one's property. Regrettably, the rights of property and contract have been seriously eroded by legislatures and by the courts. Contractual arrangements have been replaced with tort law which, in turn, has been almost completely socialized. Today, courts often award compensation to parties who have suffered no demonstrable damages while imposing liability on parties who have caused no harm.[21] In fact, modern tort law has become an even more ambitious and misguided effort to redress environmental harms than regulation; government regulators, at least, are subject to budgetary and political constraints that establish some minimal threshold of regulatory concern.[22] Civil liability is constrained by little other than the ingenuity of lawyers.

Nonetheless, reforming environmental policy is not a hopeless task—certainly not in comparison with the tasks expected of the EPA which, rather than simply being extraordinarily ambitious, are existentially impossible to accomplish. Our knowledge of how political entities operate is growing rapidly, and if we focus on the EPA as an agency, rather than on its substantive goals, our task may become simpler. We should view political risk managers as risky in their own right. We should concentrate less on the problems of political risk management, and more on the nature of political risk.

Like disease, political risk is not a necessary element of life. Like disease, political risk can be managed, treated, and cured. We seem to be getting better at it, and both old and new disciplines, ranging from economics and history to public choice theory, offer a wide variety of tools for dealing with it. Life is inherently risky, but it need not be inherently political. A world without risk may be impossible, but one without political risk is not. A world with less political risk is now being created abroad. Why not here?

Notes

1. Aaron Wildavsky, *Searching for Safety* (New Brunswick, New Jersey: Transaction Books, 1988).

2. Mary Douglas and Aaron Wildavsky, in *Risk and Culture: An Essay on the Selection of Technical and Environmental Dangers* (Berkeley, California: University of California Press, 1982), have noted that values determine what people choose to fear. Individuals focus on risks that validate and reinforce their values. Modern intellectuals, who distrust free enterprise, focus on the risks of economic and technological change and weigh natural risks much less heavily. For example, environmentalists give little attention to the massive quantities of chlorine, particulates, and acidic material spewed forth by volcanoes, while attaching great significance to the CFC residues from aerosol containers.

3. Wildavsky, *Searching for Safety*, p. 2.

4. See Sam Peltzman, *Regulation of Pharmaceutical Innovation: The 1962 Amendments* (Washington, DC: American Enterprise Institute, 1972).

5. The fact that "external" environmental costs are not always fully reflected in the price of a product or service, thus permitting the producer to ignore those social costs, is discussed below.

6. Richard B. Stewart, "Economics, Environment, and the Limits of Legal Control," *Harvard Environmental Law Review*, vol. 9 (1985), p. 10.

7. See Science Advisory Board, Environmental Protection Agency, *Reducing Risk: Setting Priorities and Strategies for Environmental Protection* (Washington, DC: EPA, 1990). This report, which contains the results of an extensive study conducted by the EPA's Science Advisory Board, has been favorably received by the EPA leadership. Perhaps the best discussion of

"managerial" and institutional reforms of the EPA is Marc K. Landy, Marc J. Roberts, and Stephen R. Thomas, *The Environmental Protection Agency: Asking the Wrong Questions* (New York: Oxford University Press, 1989).

8. See Jonathan H. Adler, "Clean Fuels, Dirty Air," in *Environmental Politics: Public Costs, Private Rewards*, Michael Greve and Fred L. Smith, Jr., eds. (New York: Praeger, 1992), p. 41.

9. See Robert Lichter and Stanley Rothman, "What Interests the Public and What Interests the Public Interest?" *Public Opinion*, vol. 6 (April/May 1983), pp. 44-48.

10. Landy, Roberts, and Thomas, *Asking the Wrong Questions*.

11. Marc K. Landy and Mary Hague, "The Coalition for Waste: Private Interests and Superfund," in Greve and Smith, *Environmental Politics*, pp. 67-88.

12. Its explicitly "partial" role and mission distinguish the Office of the Technology Advocate from existing institutions that examine the impact of EPA regulations, such as the Office of Management and Budget and the Office of Technology Assessment.

13. Sam Kazman, "Deadly Overcaution: FDA's Drug Approval Process," *Journal of Regulation and Social Cost*, vol. 1 (September 1990), pp. 35-54.

14. There is vast literature on this topic. See, for example, T.H. Tietenberg, *Emission Trading: An Exercise in Reforming Pollution Policy* (Washington, DC: Resources for the Future, 1985). Recent applied efforts have paid more attention to the nuances of these ideas and have sought to relate them to specific policy goals. See, for example, Robert Stavins, "Clean Profits: Using Economic Incentives to Protect the Environment," *Policy Review* (Spring 1989), pp. 58-63. See also my response to that article, Fred Smith, "Let's Pretend Markets," *Policy Review* (Summer 1989), pp. 94-95; and Stavins' reply in that same issue, pp. 95-96.

15. The basic arguments for and against market socialism were exchanged in the 1930s between F.A. Hayek and Oscar Lange. See F.A. Hayek, *Collectivist Economic Planning: Critical Studies on the Possibilities of Socialism* (London: Routledge Press, 1935); and F.A. Hayek, *Individualism and Economic Order* (Chicago: University of Chicago Press, 1948). See further: Donald Lavoie, *National Economic Planning: What is Left?* (Cambridge, Massachusetts: Ballinger Publishing Company, 1985).

16. See Francis S. Blake, "Tilting the Marketplace," *Regulation*, vol. 13 (Summer 1990), p. 5.

17. Robert A. Leone, Richard Startz, and Mark Farber, "The Economic Impact of the Federal Water Pollution Control Act Amendments of 1972 on the Paper and Pulp Industry," National Bureau of Economic Research, Inc., report prepared for the National Commission on Water Quality, June 15, 1975.

---

18. The exceptions, of course, are force and fraud, which are *criminal* activities.

19. F.A. Hayek, "The New Confusion about Planning," in Hayek, *New Studies in Philosophy, Politics, Economics, and the History of Ideas* (Chicago: University of Chicago Press, 1978), p. 234.

20. Ludwig von Mises, *Human Action: A Treatise on Economics*, 3rd rev. ed. (Chicago: Henry Regnery Co., 1966), pp. 657-658.

21. See Peter W. Huber, *Liability: The Legal Revolution and Its Consequences* (New York: Basic Books, 1988).

22. George L. Priest, "The New Legal Structure of Risk Control," *Daedulus* (Fall 1990), p. 208.

Labeling and Risk
The Case of Bioengineered Foods

Gregory Conko

More and more, consumers are basing their food purchases on individual preferences about food content. For many consumers this means a focus on nutrition or fat. Others care more about the methods of production, taking into consideration whether a product is kosher or organic. Some choices are made out of concern for personal health and well-being; others reflect subjective value preferences. In all cases, information on labels helps consumers select the items they prefer.

Given the choice, many consumers say they would like to know about the "genetic status" of their foods. The relative novelty of biotechnology, specifically the use of recombinant DNA techniques to modify crops and organisms, has created concern that some "bioengineered" foods are less safe, or may harm environmental quality. Some have called for a moratorium on biotechnology research, others for greater regulation. At the very least, critics argue, bioengineered products should be labeled as such.

The call for labeling seems persuasive. After all, don't consumers have the right to know what's in the very food they eat? But mandatory labeling of products is not the best way to provide consumers with information about products or even potential risks. A better solution is to let producers respond to consumer pressure in the marketplace for information that consumers want most.

Adapted from CEI's Comments to the Food and Drug Administration Regarding the Agency's Policies for Biotechnology in the Year 2000 and Beyond (Docket No. 99N-4282), April 13, 2000.

Gregory Conko

Background

The first biotechnology food products became available in 1990 with the introduction of a bioengineered enzyme used to produce cheese.[1] The Food and Drug Administration (FDA) approved recombinant bovine Somatotropin, a bioengineered growth hormone used to boost milk production in cows, in 1993.[2] And the first bioengineered plant, the Calgene Corporation's FlavrSavr slow-ripening tomato, was introduced in 1994.[3] Since that time, the FDA has evaluated and approved more than 40 new bioengineered plants.[4]

In 1992, the FDA clarified its policy on the labeling of biotech food products. The agency's policy is that foods developed from new plant varieties must be labeled if, and only if, the composition of those foods differs "significantly" from their conventional counterparts. Such differences may include the introduction of an allergen that is not present in the new plant's conventional counterpart, or the reduction in nutrients from what would be expected of the new plant's conventional counterpart. This minimal requirement is applied to all modified foods, whether developed through traditional plant-breeding methods or more advanced genetic techniques.

Producers are permitted to label bioengineered products voluntarily, and some have test-marketed affirmatively labeled products. Calgene's FlavrSavr tomato was voluntarily labeled, and was initially well-received by consumers, many of whom were willing to pay a premium for the improved flavor promised on the labels.[5] Still, most producers have heretofore refused to label their bioengineered products for fear of increased cost and consumer rejection—especially when the added trait provides benefits mainly to producers, not consumers. However, once bioengineered food products begin to add benefits for which consumers will be willing to pay a premium—and not just reduce the cost of production—producers are likely to label them voluntarily.[6]

Importantly, FDA policy on the labeling of foods derived from new plant varieties is based upon the "objective characteristics of the food product or its components rather than the fact that new development methods were used." This standard is consistent with the general scientific consensus that plants developed with new biotechnologies are not inherently more risky than those developed with conventional techniques. Over the last few decades, thousands of new plant varieties created with recombinant DNA techniques have been developed, tested, and then marketed without incident. There is no reason to believe that bioengineered food products now on the market have caused any harm to human or animal health.[7]

Nevertheless, many critics of biotechnology have challenged this policy on the labeling of bioengineered foods. In 1993, when the FDA approved recombinant Bovine Somatotropin (rbST), anti-biotechnology advocates demanded that all dairy products from cows treated with rbST be labeled as "bioengineered" or "genetically modified." When the FDA refused, activists turned their efforts to state legislatures and regulators—with variable degrees of success. More recently, however, in the wake of a successful campaign within the European Union, labeling advocates have renewed efforts to convince federal regulators and Congress.

The Harms of Mandatory Labels

When the introduction of a new plant variety (produced by recombinant DNA methods or otherwise) changes the composition of foods significantly from what would otherwise be expected from the conventional variety, the labeling of those foods to reflect that change is scientifically defensible. But because recombinant DNA techniques themselves pose no apparent danger to human or animal health, a mandatory label on all bioengineered foods can not be justified. If consumers want the information, it will be provided in the marketplace.

In 1996, the United States Second Circuit Court of Appeals, in the case of *International Dairy Foods Association, et al. v. Amestoy*,[8] noted that a labeling mandate not grounded in a product's

Gregory Conko

measurable characteristics raises serious constitutional concerns. The court held that food labeling cannot be mandated simply because some people would like to have the information. That decision held unconstitutional a Vermont statute and companion regulations requiring that "[i]f rbST has been used in the production of milk or a milk product for retail sale in [Vermont], the retail milk or milk product shall be labeled as such."[9]

Because the state of Vermont could not demonstrate that its interest in compelling acknowledgment of rbST represented anything more than satisfying consumer curiosity, it could not compel milk producers to include that information on product labels. In the words of the court,

> Absent some indication that this information bears on a reasonable concern for human health or safety or some other sufficiently substantial governmental concern, the manufacturers cannot be compelled to disclose it. Instead, *those consumers interested in such information should exercise the power of their purses by buying products from manufacturers who voluntarily reveal it.* (emphasis added)

In other words, to be constitutional, labeling mandates must be based in science and confined to requiring disclosure of information that is relevant to health or nutrition.

Of course, many consumers care about more than the safety and nutritional content of the food they buy. Other information about food products can be extremely important to consumers due to religious, ethical, and/or other strong personal values. Such information may include certification of kosher or organic production, or other characteristics pertaining to process attributes. Insofar as consumers truly care about the techniques used to produce their food, there is an incentive for companies to respond by providing it.

For instance, if many consumers want products free of any bioengineered ingredients, companies that meet this need can gain market share by advertising this fact. The growth of the organic food industry, despite the lack of formal labeling requirements (as of yet) is a testament to how this process works when consumers demand products made in a particular manner.

Information Overload

One often-neglected problem of mandatory labels is that of "information overload" or the "crowding out" of important information. Many consumers turn to food labels to get important information about such things as nutrient and fat content, the presence of certain allergens, or even proper storage and preparation information. Each of these bits of information can have a material effect on their health. The appearance on a food product label of too much information about materially irrelevant facts—those not pertaining to legitimate issues of health—can make it more difficult for consumers to locate important facts about the foods they consume.

Indeed, the appearance of too much information increases the risk that consumers will pay less attention to individual messages within labels, making it more difficult to transmit information regarding real hazards.[10] Federal laws mandate that all sorts of information be included with over-the-counter and prescription drugs, but how many people actually take the time to read every page of the tightly printed inserts? As a Michigan Appeals Court noted in *Dunn v. Lederle Laboratories*, "[m]aking consumers account mentally for trivia or guard against risks that are not likely to occur imposes a very real societal cost."

Though there is a danger of requiring too much information, some consumers will have an interest in information about the development and/or processing of foods. It is important, then, that the FDA abstain from micromanaging the specific content of food

Gregory Conko

product labels. Where consumer demand is strong enough, niche markets will emerge to provide consumers with desired information in a format that they find easy to use. When it comes to information about consumer products, especially information relating to personal values, one size does not fit all—consumer preferences are not homogeneous. To grant consumers a real choice, the FDA need not mandate that specific information appear on labels; it need only protect the right of producers to make accurate, truthful statements.

Competition and Information

The importance of private, voluntary labeling schemes should not be understated. Much research indicates that voluntary labeling and advertising transmits useful and important information to consumers in a format they find easy to understand.[11] Indeed, market competition among producers for providing demanded information can even drive producers to make better products. Studies of voluntary food health claims, conducted by researchers at the US Federal Trade Commission, found that, when food manufacturers were permitted to mention diet-disease relationships on their package labels, consumers began to reduce their dietary intake of fat, saturated fat, and cholesterol, and to increase fiber intake. Moreover, the resulting competition among manufacturers to provide this information encouraged manufacturers to make healthier products.[12]

Mandatory-labeling advocates argue that the general resistance by producers of bioengineered foods to label products voluntarily represents a failure of the market to provide information that consumers want. However, it is not clear that, in the case of bioengineered foods, the market has failed to supply demanded information. Nor is it clear that a government mandate to affirmatively label bioengineered products will provide better or more useful information. Many real-world examples show that market forces are fully capable of supplying information about process attributes for food products that consumers truly demand. Consider two real-world examples: kosher and organic foods.

For religious purposes, many Jewish people purchase foods that have been processed according to the Kashrut, or kosher, dietary rules. There are a large number of private kosher certification organizations that keep to varying degrees of Kashrut strictness, and some purchasers of kosher products seek out only foods approved by specific certifying organizations.[13] In this way, kosher certification provides a range of information useful to consumers. The existence of competing certification organizations provides a level of consumer choice that would be impossible under a government-imposed, one-size-fits-all labeling scheme.

Voluntary labeling within the organic food industry represents an even closer analogue to the process-based information now requested of bioengineered foods. Many people believe that organically produced foods are, in some way, healthier than conventionally produced foods, and they seek out products that are labeled organic because organic agriculture shuns synthetic chemical pesticides, herbicides, and fertilizers. Even though there doesn't appear to be a strong consumer demand for products that are *certified* organic (as opposed to self-identified),[14] some 33 private organic-certifying organizations have sprung up in the United States alone, to compliment government and international standard-setting bodies. And while there has been a concerted voluntary movement within the organic industry to codify standards for "organic" certification,[15] a move by the US government to create a single, national standard failed to satisfy many in the organic food industry.[16] The Organic Trade Association lamented that "the proposed federal regulations will actually be weaker than the current decentralized regulation practices."[17]

The organic example is an important one within the context of this paper, as many organic purists insist that foods produced with bioengineered materials can not be considered organic.[18] Consequently, to ensure that they are purchasing only foods produced without bioengineering, consumers need only look for an appropriate organic certification. Furthermore, voluntary labeling and certification of non-bioengineered foods specifically is already being pursued. In 1999, one of the largest organic-certifying organizations formed a private certification company established to meet "growing demand by consumers, governments and the food industry for rigorous and ethical third-party certification of food and fiber production."[19] And members of the organic and "natural" food industry in the United Kingdom formed an organization known as Genetic Food Alert, to register food producers that do not use bioengineered products.[20] Each of these examples demonstrates that, when consumers truly demand certain types of information, the market usually finds a way of supplying it—even in cases where that demand is not extensive.

One measure of robust consumer demand is willingness to pay. Because certification and labeling are not free, consumers in these examples demonstrate that they are, in fact, willing to pay for the information they receive. To the extent that a legitimate consumer demand for information about the genetic status of food products currently exists, it comes primarily from consumers wishing to purchase foods that are not bioengineered. Requiring producers of bioengineered foods to label their products as such shifts the enormous cost of providing this information from those who are demanding it onto consumers who are not—a position that hardly seems reasonable or equitable.

Conclusion

Recombinant DNA techniques have already been used to develop crop plants with traits that increase yields and that allow farmers to reduce their use of synthetic pesticides and herbicides.[21] The next generation of products promises to provide even greater benefits to consumers, such as enhanced nutritional value and improved medicines. But a labeling requirement for these products could impose high costs on producers and consumers, without producing any corresponding benefits. Ultimately, the monetary costs of a labeling mandate could all but preclude many consumers who are indifferent to genetic status from sharing in the vast potential benefits of the bioengineering revolution.

Leaving labeling to private markets encourages firms to differentiate themselves by providing information about their products that actually matters to consumers. At the same time, economic pressures encourage producers to present this information in the most direct and accessible manner possible. The only real role for the federal government in this enterprise is to guard against outright fraud. Whether the issue is biotechnology or some other food characteristics, the rest should be left to the market.

Notes

1. James H. Maryanski, "FDA's Policy for Foods Developed by Biotechnology," in *Genetically Modified Foods: Safety Issues*, Engel, Takeoka, and Teranishi, eds., American Chemical Society, Symposium Series No. 605 (1995), pp. 12-22.

2. Center for Veterinary Medicine of the US Food and Drug Administration, "BST Update," *CVM Update,* March 21, 1996.

3. Center for Food Safety and Applied Nutrition of the US Food and Drug Administration, *Biotechnology of Food*, FDA Backgrounder, May 18, 1994.

4. Food and Drug Administration, "Notice: Biotechnology in the Year 2000 and Beyond; Public Meetings," *Federal Register*, Docket No. 99N-4282; 57 FR 57470, October 25, 1999.

5. Karen K. Marshall, "What's in a Label?" *AgBioForum*, vol. 1, no. 1 (Summer 1998), pp. 35-37. It should be noted that, while sales of the FlavrSavr tomato eventually faded, this is usually attributed to the use of inferior tomato varieties, rather than rejection of bioengineering.

6. Peter W.B. Phillips and Grant Isaac, "GMO Labeling: Threat or Opportunity?" *AgBioForum*, vol. 1, no. 1 (Summer 1998), pp. 25-30.

7. David L. Aaron, "Testimony of Ambassador David L. Aaron, Under Secretary for International Trade, US Department of Commerce, before the Senate Committee on Finance," October 7, 1999; and Mark Silbergeld, "Testimony of

Mark Silbergeld, Co-Director of the Washington Office of Consumers Union, Before the Committee On Agriculture, United States Senate," October 7, 1999. Even Silbergeld, a leading critic of bioengineered foods, admitted in his testimony that "there is no evidence of harm to consumers."

8. 92 F.3d 67 (2nd Cir. 1996).

9. Vt. Stat. Ann. tit. 6, § 2754(c), overturned by the *International Dairy Foods Association* decision.

10. See, for example, J. Paul Frantz, et al., "Potential Problems Associated with Overusing Warnings," Proceedings of the 7th International Conference on Product Safety Research (Washington, DC: European Consumer Safety Association and the US Consumer Product Safety Commission, 1999); Aaron D. Twerski, et al., "The Use and Abuse of Warnings in Product Liability—Design Defect Litigation Comes of Age," *Cornell Law Review*, vol. 61, no. 4 (1976), pp. 514-517; and Aaron D. Twerski, "From Risk-Utility to Consumer Expectation: Enhancing the Role of Judicial Screening in Product Liability Litigation," *Hofstra Law Review*, vol. 11 (1983), pp. 861-935.

11. See, for example, George Stigler, "The Economics of Information," *Journal of Political Economy*, vol. 69 (1961), pp. 213-225; and Pauline M. Ippolito, "Consumer Protection Economics: A Selected Survey," in *Empirical Approaches to Consumer Protection Economics*, Pauline M. Ippolito and David T. Scheffman, eds. (Washington, DC: Federal Trade Commission, 1986), pp. 1-33.

12. Pauline M. Ippolito and Alan D. Mathios, *Information and Advertising Policy: A Study of Fat and Cholesterol Consumption in the United States, 1977-1990*, Bureau of Economics Staff Report (Washington, DC: Federal Trade Commission, September 1996); and Pauline M. Ippolito and Alan D. Mathios, *Health Claims in Advertising and Labeling: A Study of the Cereal Market*, Bureau of Economics Staff Report (Washington, DC: Federal Trade Commission, 1989).

13. See, for example, Michael I. Krauss, "Loosening the FDA's Drug Certification Monopoly: Implications for Tort Law and Consumer Welfare," *George Mason Law Review*, vol. 4, no. 3 (Spring 1996), pp. 457-483.

14. Carole Sugarman, "Organic? Industry is Way Ahead of Government," *Washington Post*, December 31, 1997.

15. Organic Trade Association, *American Organic Standards: Guidelines for the Organic Industry*, compiled by James A. Riddle, Emily Brown Rosen, and Lynn S. Coody (Greenfield, Massachusetts: Organic Trade Association, 1999), p. 19.

16. See, for example, Sugarman, "Organic?"; and Anon. "Organic farming: Let's keep it clean," *The Economist*, April 17, 1999, pp. 34-35.

17. Organic Trade Association, "Organic Standards At Risk," press release, January 27, 1998.

18. Organic Trade Association, *American Organic Standards*, p. 10.

19. Genetic ID, "New Company Forms to Provide Enhanced Consumer Safeguards for Food," press release, January 28, 1999.

20. Genetic Food Alert, "GM-Free Registration Scheme for Businesses and Products," current draft as of January 11, 1999, www.essential-trading.co.uk/genetix.htm.

21. See, for example, Leonard P. Gianessi and Janet E. Carpenter, *Agricultural Technology: Insect Control Benefits* (Washington, DC: National Center for Food and Agriculture Policy, 1999); and Economic Research Service of the US Department of Agriculture, *Bioengineered Crops for Pest Management*, October 27, 1999, www.econ.ag.gov/whatsnew/issues/biotech/.

A Risk-Risk Approach to Climate Change

Fred L. Smith, Jr.

Former Environmental Protection Agency Administrator William Reilly once quipped that his agency had a "Ready! Fire! Aim!" approach to policy. The global warming debate provides ample evidence that this tendency remains alive and well. Political activists and media spokesmen reinforce this "act first, think later" bias by emphasizing the possible risks of global warming, while providing little information about the possible risks of the policies proposed to head off such warming. This cannot result in sound policy, as the debate over the United Nations climate treaty, the Kyoto Protocol, makes clear.

In the face of numerous uncertainties associated with climate change, how should society act? How can we best review the evidence and decide the appropriate course of action in an area as complex as global warming? The use of energy *might* be warming the earth. That warming *might* produce catastrophic results. We *might* be able to prevent warming by an aggressive global carbon-withdrawal policy. Finally, the cost and effectiveness of policies aimed at restricting energy use and stabilizing anthropogenic greenhouse gas emissions (a "prevention" strategy) *might* be superior to those of policies aimed at encouraging economic and technological growth, and thereby improving our ability to ride out whatever risks global warming *might* entail (a "resiliency" strategy).

Adapted from "The Role of Opportunity Costs in the Global Warming Debate" in *The Costs of Kyoto*, Jonathan H. Adler, ed. (Washington, DC: Competitive Enterprise Institute, 1997).

Of course, one or more of these statements *might not* be true. How can we know? How should we decide? The Precautionary Principle seems to answer the question decisively—even in the face of scientific uncertainty, we should act to head-off potential destructive trends. But this principle resolves nothing. Its attractiveness masks a simplistic world in which the costs of delaying or blocking economic and technological change are assigned zero weight. The implicit presumption is that the risks of innovation vastly outweigh the risks of stagnation. This presumption has little theoretical or empirical validity, merely disguising a reactionary preference for the *status quo*. For the wealthy elites comprising the core of the environmental movement, such policies may seem ideal, but the world's poor may have different preferences.

An alternative to the Precautionary Principle is provided by Statistical Decision Theory. This approach argues that in making decisions under uncertainty, one should test the validity of the apocalyptic global warming hypothesis: the belief that the world is warming, that this warming will be catastrophic, and that we can effectively prevent such warming at reasonable cost. To do so, we should engage in careful modeling and assiduously collect data that would confirm or deny the validity of the models. At each period, there are three choices: Accept the global warming catastrophe theory and act accordingly, reject it, or collect more data. How do we decide? We must estimate the expected consequences—the costs and benefits—of each course.

The consequences of delay are obvious—we may incur higher costs later (an ounce of prevention is worth a pound of cure). Those consequences must be compared with those of either accepting or rejecting the global warming agenda. It would be nice always to get it right, but that is unlikely. There are two potential errors that might be made: a Type I error (the risk that the global warming advocates have it right and society ignores their advice) and a Type II error (the risk that the global warming advocates are wrong and we dampen global prosperity). Vice President Al Gore, Greenpeace, and the renewable energy industry have done much to highlight the potential costs of a Type I error. Indeed, in his widely publicized book, *Earth in the Balance*, Vice President Gore argued that western society's emissions of greenhouse gases constituted an "ecological Kristallnacht"—a clear signal that mankind must move rapidly to curtail fossil fuel consumption. Gore argued that those critical of his policies are morally akin to those who remained passive as the Nazis seized power throughout Europe.

Yet Type II errors—embarking upon a drastic fossil fuel reduction program even though the risks posed by warming are minimal—also must receive consideration. Over time, we gain knowledge over the likelihood that human activities are or are not causing global warming (and the extent and speed of any expected shifts). We also become more aware of the consequences of such a warming trend and whether it is likely to advance or retard human welfare. Research can give us greater certainty as to whether the measures proposed to reduce man's climatic influence are—or are not—likely to prove effective. The theory suggests we continue collecting data until the value of the knowledge gained (the greater certainty of the difference between the expected consequences of Type I and Type II errors) is less than the costs of further delay. At that time, we would either accept or reject the global warming hypothesis and respond accordingly.

This is not being done—and it is not easy to do—but it does offer a rational approach to thinking through a complex issue. At present, almost everything is in doubt. The science is uncertain, the need for haste unproven. We're not even sure whether warming is good or bad! There is substantial evidence that a carbon-dioxide-enriched atmosphere would produce many benefits, from less severe winters to longer and more productive growing seasons. Whether climatic change is best addressed by a prevention or adaptation strategy has received almost no attention. Rather, an attempt has been made to rush to judgement—to act rather than to think. The climate may be changing, it may be for the worse, restricting energy use might reduce the threat—QED!

We deserve better. In a world in which information is never perfect, but opportunity costs are omnipresent, environmental policy must be determined in a risk-risk framework. We must consider both Type I and Type II errors; we must consider whether prevention or adaptation offers a superior response. We should be concerned about the risks of global warming, but we should also be concerned about the risks of global warming policy.

The "Science" of Global Warming: Is it Happening?

The first stage of the decision process is to review the science of global warming. In climate science, some facts are agreed upon, others are not. Among the accepted facts are: The climate of the earth depends upon the energy received largely from the sun via radiation, the amount of that heat retained by the earth because of the greenhouse effect, and the extent to which that heat is distributed vertically and horizontally around the world by air and water currents. Were radiation the only impact on our planet, the earth would be too cold for life. Were radiation and the greenhouse effect the only influences, the earth would be too hot. Additional impacts include convection which moves heat from the earth's surface to the troposphere where it is radiated into space (via outward longwave radiation). This latter effect reduces the "raw" greenhouse effect and makes our planet habitable.

Most also agree that the concentrations of carbon dioxide and other greenhouse gases in the atmosphere have increased significantly over the last century. (Water vapor, which constitutes the vast bulk of all greenhouse gases at 90-plus percent, is assumed to be constant, although little data exists on this topic.) Carbon dioxide has increased by 28 percent over this period, mostly in the last few decades; other greenhouse-gas concentrations have increased as well. Concurrently, most scientists believe there has been a real, but slight (0.5 degrees C), increase in global temperature. However, human-induced increases in carbon dioxide levels cannot easily be linked to this temperature increase. Most of the observed warming (approximately 70 percent) occurred before 1940, while most of the greenhouse-gas buildup occured after 1940. Other trends, of course, may have obscured the warming impact, but the issue remains unsettled. Many temperature measurements are from urban areas that were once rural, biasing the temperature records upward. The less biased and more accurate source of temperature data, the satellite record available since 1979, shows no temperature increase. Efforts to relate model predictions to empirical measurements continue, with minimal success.

The computer models which suggest serious temperature changes are evolving rapidly, but still remain crude approximations of the complexities of the energy and material transfer systems that determine weather. Current computing capacity limits the "unit" of analysis to a very large volume of the atmosphere, rendering the models less useful for regional weather analysis. Moreover, the treatment of factors known to be key to climate remains weak. For example, the variability of solar radiation, which some believe may well explain most of the temperature variation of the last century, is largely ignored. Water, which scientists increasingly recognize as the critical variable in the climate determination game, is handled in a simplistic fashion. Dynamic interaction effects, such as how warming might impact upon the amount, distribution and state (liquid, gaseous, solid) of water in the atmosphere, are also addressed in rather rigid ways. Some have argued that the additional surface warming suggested by carbon dioxide increases would increase ground-level moisture levels and increase the strength of convection currents which move heat from the surface to the troposphere. The efficiency of out-radiation of heat is influenced strongly by the dryness of the tropospheric air masses. If the overall impact of surface level warming is a less moist troposphere, then much of any initial greenhouse warming impact might be offset; if the effect is a moister upper atmosphere, then we might anticipate greater warming. Current models simulate these critical relations only imperfectly. For such reasons, it is quite possible that humanity's impact on the climate system is not all that severe. If so, there is little reason to engage in any further discourse.

The Economics of Global Warming: Should We Worry?

The second phase of the decision process addresses the "so what" question. Even if the scientific evidence were to suggest that human-induced global warming were a certainty, this would decide little. It is not temperature change *per se* that triggers the global warming concern, but rather views as to how such changes will affect our planet and human civilization. Warmer weather will certainly have benefits—lower heating bills in the winter and greater agricultural productivity—but some argue it will also increase the frequency and/or severity of hurricanes and floods. Hurricane Andrew and the Mississippi-Missouri floods were disasters of unanticipated magnitude, and we should clearly be concerned if the frequency of such disasters is likely to increase. Here, however, the evidence remains so inconclusive that even the report of the UN Intergovernmental Panel on Climate Change stated, "Overall, there is no evidence that extreme weather events, or climate variability, has increased, in a global sense, through the 20th century, although data and analyses are poor and not comprehensive."

In fact, warmer weather may well be better weather. Evidence for this may be found in the terminology used by the English climatologist Hubert H. Lamb to label the two warmest periods of the last ten thousand years: the Climate Optimum around 5000 to 1000 BC and the Little Climate Optimum around 800 to 1200 AD. Recent historical research by Dr. Thomas Gale Moore provides further evidence that warmer weather correlates well with better times.

Such findings are compatible with current climate-change theories which suggest that if warming occurs, it will largely occur at night, in the winter, and at higher latitudes. Such a warming pattern would likely lengthen growing seasons and, by reducing temperature variations over time, tend to reduce extreme weather events. Furthermore, higher levels of carbon dioxide increase plant growth and thus increase agricultural output. Thus, it is not clear that global warming is something that should be prevented, even if it were easy to do at an affordable cost.

In any event, the existing computer models (the basis of most global warming claims) suggest slow response rates to any changes in carbon dioxide levels, which implies that quick action now would have little impact on climate for many decades. One recent study suggested that delays on the order of a decade or so would have little impact on the temperatures that might be expected in the late 21st century. Since discontinuing any political program is extremely difficult, we should be very careful about locking ourselves into what may well be an unnecessary program. The science of global warming provides little support that global warming is clearly upon us, that it will prove decisively harmful, or that urgent action is required. That is, the answer to the phase two question, "Should we worry?" is "Probably not."

The Politics of Global Warming: Would Policies Work?

The final decision-process issue deals with political feasibility. Even if global warming were to occur and it were harmful to the United States, or the world at large, the question remains as to whether any viable political strategy exists to prevent it. Greenhouse gases are linked closely to the use of carbon-based fuels. For the foreseeable future, carbon-based fuel represents the only form of energy useful for mobile sources. Electricity, in principle, could be produced via nuclear plants, but the environmental establishment would vigorously oppose any move toward greater reliance on nuclear energy; ditto hydropower. Even if the United States were somehow to reduce carbon-based energy use, it would do little good unless most other nations do likewise. Is this likely, or even feasible? Not really. First, note that no agreement in history approximates the complexity of the proposed Kyoto agreement. Nations would have to control the household energy budgets of their citizens, monitor all industrial and agricultural activities, and restrict mobility. America has been very reluctant to penalize energy consumption via gas taxes; why will the global warming proposals face an easier time?

Moreover, the United States and the rest of the developed world are projected to comprise an even smaller fraction of the world greenhouse-gas emission budget. If we are to reduce greenhouse gases, the developing world also must reduce its projected use of energy. For such reasons, great pressures are being placed upon developing nations to ratify the Kyoto global warming treaty. Western governments promise technological and economic aid to offset the costs of reduced energy use; however, the amounts required to improve living standards or suppressed economic growth seem unattainable. Indeed, a world made poorer by restrictive energy policies seems far more likely to be less generous than the world of today. Certainly, private capital flows (the dominant source of international aid today) would decline as world economic growth contracts, were significant restraints on energy use adopted.

Nonetheless, many countries have endorsed the Kyoto Protocol. Yet while it is easy to sign a treaty, it is far harder to monitor its compliance. Developing countries have little ability or reason to comply with complex carbon-reduction policies. The sophisticated regulatory and tax arrangements which make it possible for energy regulators in the United States and Europe to monitor and enforce current anti-energy-use laws are weak to nonexistent in the Third World. Efforts there to raise the price of market energy might simply lead to increased reliance on non-market derived fuels such as wood and dung. These fuels would be even more difficult to monitor and could produce *even more* carbon dioxide than the coal, oil, or natural gas displaced. Such traditional "renewable" fuels also contribute to other environmental problems, such as indoor air pollution, a real concern in the developing world. The argument noted above that such problems could be offset by economic aid or transfers of "environmentally friendly" technologies from developed to developing countries is naïve. The world is today far too poor for naked wealth transfers to offset a slowdown in growth.

Foreign aid, in any event, has largely been a failure. Too often, it becomes nothing more than a shift of funds from the poor in the developed world to the rich in the developing world. Too often, such political wealth transfers are wasted in symbolic or pork barrel projects, reducing rather than enhancing the wealth of these nations. Much of the environmental arguments for wealth transfers today are little more than a recycling of arguments raised years ago. Then it was argued the South was poor because the North was rich; the solution was to transfer wealth from the North to the South. The global warming debate now incorporates a green version of that same idea.

The dismal history of international agreements suggests that rhetorical treaties rarely ensure realistic results. Note that any global energy reduction treaty would be akin to a super-OPEC which in its own way for its own purposes has long sought to moderate energy use. From time to time, largely when war or national policy has disrupted energy markets, OPEC has approximated this energy restriction role. Mostly, however, OPEC has failed. Although the OPEC members would all have benefited from actual curtailment of energy output, their self-interest encouraged each of them to produce more energy. The result was that while all OPEC members expressed support for the energy curtailment program, most simultaneously expanded output. The reasons for cooperative energy reduction policies are far less compelling for non-OPEC countries.

Non-OPEC nations have no common interest in energy-use reduction; thus, one would expect even less success with a Kyoto-style
agreement.

This may be a good thing; people may be far better off if
the Kyoto agreement fails than if it succeeds. After all, any developing nation able to exercise effective control over the household
energy budgets of its citizenry would have massive power indeed.
Many nations in the world are just emerging from decades of
government abuse, especially abuse to those subpopulations not
represented in the ruling class. Have the risks of granting politicians a renewed license to exercise moral power over the citizenry
been considered? Would one really wish to grant a ruling minority
in a balkanized nation life-and-death power over energy use by their
historic rivals?

These thoughts aside, it remains the case that an agreement
that omits the developing world will do little to stem the growth in
greenhouse gases and thus to address the perceived threat of global
warming. Most of the greenhouse gases produced to date have come
from developed nations. But energy use in the developed world has
plateaued. All projections indicate that in the 21st century, the major increases in these gases will come from the developing world.
And, while we in the developed world might, at high cost, adapt to
a virtual reality world of minimal increased energy use, we start
from a very real level of comfort. The people of the developing
world do not. If they are to improve their standards of living, they
must consume far more energy than they do today; that increase for
the foreseeable future will rely heavily on carbon-based fuels. For
such reasons, the developing world has been excluded from the first
round of Kyoto. This exclusion is understandable and justifiable;
yet it makes meaningless the sacrifices urged upon the United States
and the other developed nations.

Under current conditions, any global warming treaty would
resemble an "All Pain, No Gain" energy diet. Even if all the fears

of the global warming advocates are conceded, it remains doubtful that a carbon-withdrawal policy would make sense.

The Superiority of Resiliency

Regardless of whether global warming is real or not—much less whether proposed control policies will prove effective—the point remains that we are right to be concerned over the economic consequences of potential climate catastrophes. What course of action should we pursue? Those favoring expanded political control of the world economy seek to short-circuit this process, arguing that only a political approach, and then only one focused on stopping change—not adapting to it—offers any true "solution." In the alternative, there is much that can be done to make society more robust, more able to overcome whatever future climate (or other) risks our world may face.

Whether the future will be warmer or colder, wetter or drier, stormier or more tranquil—some risks will increase and others will decline. Hampering the ability of private markets to respond to changing conditions serves no one's interests. Indeed, it can be destructive. Stanford University's Stephen Schneider suggests that those who oppose precipitous action to avert global climate change are willing to run an uncontrolled experiment on the only planet that we have. Yet Schneider and those who join him in calling for dramatic emission reductions are all too willing to run an uncontrolled experiment on our only civilization. Thus, the proper question to ask is: In the face of change, should we try to freeze the world and eliminate change? Or should we improve our abilities to adjust, to adapt, to an ever-changing world? America and the world will certainly face severe risks in the future—whether these will be climatic, tectonic, biologic, or political is unclear. Since we cannot be sure which risks will prove dominant, the case for improving our generalized strengths, for becoming smarter and wealthier, is decisive.

Consider the following example: Violent tropical storms occur in both America and Asia. When a hurricane occurs in Florida, people are alerted early, they hunker down or move out of the way, the widespread availability of private automobiles gives them the mobility to do so, their wealth and that of our society gives them the ability to incur the expenses of such a relocation, and the communication and technological infrastructure of our nation provide them targeted and timely warning. The storms in Bangladesh are not dissimilar; yet, Bangladesh lacks the wealth, the communication and technological infrastructure, and the mobility needed to respond to such risks. The risks are the same but the adaptability of our two countries is very different. The results reflect this. In the United States, very few people die from climatic disturbances. In Bangladesh and the poorer areas of the world, the fatality lists are tragically long. Is it better to divert wealth to reduce an already-low likelihood that current fossil fuel use might increase the severity or frequency of storms, or would we achieve more by assisting these poorer nations to gain the greater wealth and technological skills which make such climatic disturbances relatively unimportant to our own societies? This is the question on which the global warming debate should focus.

Those favoring global warming policies often suggest that minimally we adopt a "no regrets" policy—do those things that should be done in any event. To this group, of course, this implies the reduction of America's "wasteful" use of energy and materials, moving toward "sustainable development." But a more useful view of the "no regrets" policy would focus on reforming the political process and freeing up the economic forces that expand society's choices. This would involve a series of policy initiatives such as deregulation, elimination of government subsidy programs in the energy sector, and privatization of government enterprises which inhibit our ability to offset natural disasters. We should eliminate the political preferences and subsidies that encourage certain fuels over more efficient alternatives. We should deregulate electricity generation and transmission and thereby allow the most efficient (and typically least-polluting) firms to expand output. We should remove regulatory barriers that limit innovation and technological advance. And, we should encourage such free-market reforms throughout the world through trade liberalization and the elimination of wealth-transfer programs which perpetuate socialist policies. The policies that are best for the ecology of the earth are those that are best for the economy of the earth. No policy that harms people can help our planet. That fact should be the bases of all environmental programs.

There are risks of global warming. Yet these risks should be balanced against the risks of proposed global warming policies. The greatest risk of carbon-withdrawal policies is that they will fail to achieve any positive results while imposing major costs on the world's economy. These risks are likely to fall most heavily on the poor in the developed and developing nations. The risk of starving the world of energy is all too likely to be a world of starving people. The costs of Kyoto are all too real. Once realized, it is likely that few elected policymakers will rush to jump on the global warming bandwagon.

About the Authors

❖ ❖ ❖

Jonathan H. Adler is a senior fellow in environmental policy at the Competitive Enterprise Institute where he oversaw the environmental studies program from 1994 to 1998. He is the author of *Environmentalism at the Crossroads* (1995) and editor of *The Costs of Kyoto: Climate Change Policy and Its Implications* (1997).

Gregory Conko is Director of Food Safety Policy at the Competitive Enterprise Institute.

Michael De Alessi is the director of the Center for Private Conservation, a project of the Competitive Enterprise Institute, and the author of *Fishing for Solutions* (1998).

James V. DeLong is vice president and general counsel of the National Legal Center for the Public Interest. A former adjunct scholar at the Competitive Enterprise Institue, he is the author of *Property Matters* (1997).

Paul Georgia is an environmental research associate at the Competitive Enterprise Institute and the managing editor of the bi-weekly climate change policy newsletter *May Cooler Heads Prevail.*

Urs Kreuter is an adjunct scholar at the Competitive Enterprise Institute and a member of the advisory board of the Center for Private Conservation. He is assistant professor in rangeland ecology and management at Texas A&M University.

Robert H. Nelson is a senior fellow in environmental studies at the Competitive Enterprise Institute and a professor in the School of Public Affairs at the University of Maryland.

James M. Sheehan is a student at the Fuqua School of Business at Duke University. He was a research associate at the Competitive Enterprise Institute from 1991 to 1999, and is the author of *Global Greens* (1998).

Randy Simmons is a professor of political science and director of the Institute of Political Economy at Utah State University. He was a visiting scholar at the Competitive Enterprise Institute in 1989.

Fred L. Smith, Jr. is the founder and President of the Competitive Enterprise Institute and the editor (with Michael Greve) of *Environmental Politics: Public Costs, Private Rewards* (1992).

Robert J. Smith is senior environmental scholar at the Center for Private Conservation, a project of the Competitive Enterprise Institute.

Ike C. Sugg is executive director of the Exotic Wildlife Association in Kerrville, Texas, and an adjunct scholar at the Competitive Enterprise Institute, where he was a fellow in wildlife and land-use policy from 1990 to 1998.

Selected Bibliography

Adler, Jonathan H. *Environmentalism at the Crossroads: Green Activism in America* (Washington, DC: Capital Research Center, 1995).

----------. "Faux Market Environmentalism," *Regulation*, vol. 23, no. 1 (2000), pp. 54-57.

----------. "Swamp Rules: The End of Federal Wetland Regulation?" *Regulation*, vol. 22, no. 2 (1999), pp. 11-16.

Anderson, Terry L. *Breaking the Environmental Policy Gridlock* (Stanford, California: Hoover Institution Press, 1997).

----------. "The New Resource Economics: Old Ideas and New Applications," *American Journal of Agricultural Economics*, vol. 64, no. 5 (December 1982), pp. 928-934.

Anderson, Terry L., and Donald R. Leal. *Free Market Environmentalism* (San Francisco: Pacific Research Institute for Public Policy and Westview Press, 1991).

Anderson, Terry L., and Pamela Snyder. *Water Markets: Priming the Invisible Pump* (Washington, DC: Cato Institute, 1997).

Baden, John A., and Donald R. Leal, eds. *The Yellowstone Primer: Land and Resource Management in the Greater Yellowstone Ecosystem* (San Francisco: Pacific Research Institute for Public Policy, 1990).

Baden, John A., and Richard Stroup. *Bureaucracy vs. the Environment: The Environmental Costs of Bureaucratic Government* (Ann Arbor: University of Michigan Press, 1981).

Bailey, Ronald, ed. *Earth Report 2000: The True State of the Planet Revisited* (New York: McGraw-Hill, 1999).

----------, ed. *The True State of the Planet* (New York: The Free Press, 1995).

Bast, Joseph L., Peter J. Hill, and Richard C. Rue. *Eco-Sanity: A Common-Sense Guide to Environmentalism* (Lanham, Maryland: Madison Books, 1994).

Bernstam, Mikhail S. *The Wealth of Nations and the Environment* (London: Institute for Economic Affairs, 1991).

Block, Walter. *Economics and the Environment: A Reconciliation* (Vancouver, British Columbia: The Fraser Institute, 1990).

Brubaker, Elizabeth. *Property Rights in the Defence of Nature* (Toronto, Ontario: Earthscan Publications Ltd., 1995).

Dales, J.H. *Pollution, Property, and Prices* (Toronto, Ontario: University of Toronto Press, 1968).

Deacon, Robert T., and M. Bruce Johnson, eds. *Forestlands: Public and Private* (San Francisco: Pacific Institute for Policy Research, 1985).

De Alessi, Michael. *Fishing for Solutions* (London: IEA Environment Unit, 1998).

Demsetz, Harold. "Toward a Theory of Property Rights," *American Economic Review* (May 1967), pp. 347-360.

Hess, Karl, Jr. *Visions Upon the Land: Man and Nature on the Western Range* (Covelo, California: Island Press, 1992).

Huffman, James. "Protecting the Environment from Orthodox Environmentalism," *Harvard Journal of Public Policy*, vol. 15, no. 2 (Spring 1992), pp. 349-370.

Meiners, Roger E., and Andrew P. Morriss. *The Common Law and the Environment* (Lanham, Maryland: Rowman & Littlefield, 2000).

Nelson, Robert H. *Public Land and Private Rights: The Failure of Scientific Management* (Lanham, Maryland: Rowman & Littlefield, 1995).

O'Toole, Randal. *Reforming the Forest Service* (Washington, DC: Island Press, 1988).

Osterfeld, David. *Prosperity versus Planning: How Government Stifles Economic Growth* (New York: Oxford University Press, 1992).

Rothbard, Murray N. "Law, Property Rights, and Air Pollution," *Cato Journal*, vol. 2, no. 1 (Spring 1982), pp. 55-100.

Scarlett, Lynn. "Evolutionary Ecology: A New Environmental Vision," *Reason* (May 1996), pp. 20-26.

Sheehan, James M. *Global Greens: Inside the International Environmental Establishment* (Washington, DC: Capital Research Center, 1998).

Simon, Julian L. *The State of Humanity* (Cambridge: Blackwell Publishers, 1995).

Smith, Fred L., Jr. "A Free-Market Environmental Program," *Cato Journal*, vol. 11, no. 3 (1992), pp. 457-475.

Smith, Fred L., Jr., and Michael S. Greve, eds. *Environmental Politics: Public Costs, Private Rewards* (New York: Praeger, 1992).

Smith, Robert J. "Private Solutions to Conservation Problems," in Tyler Cowen, ed., *The Theory of Market Failure: A Critical Examination* (Fairfax, Virginia: George Mason University Press, 1988), pp. 341-360.

----------. "Privatizing the Environment," *Policy Review* (Spring 1982), pp. 11-50.

----------. "Special Report: The Public Benefits of Private Conservation," *Environmental Quality: The 15th Annual Report of the Council on Environmental Quality* (Washington, DC: Government Printing Office, 1986), pp. 363-429.

Stroup, Richard. "Controlling Earth's Response: Market or Socialism?" *Population and Environment: A Journal of Interdisciplinary Studies* (Spring 1991), pp. 265-284.

Sugg, Ike C. "Caught in the Act: Evaluating the Endangered Species Act," *Cumberland Law Review*, vol. 24 (1993), pp. 1-54.

Sugg, Ike C., and Urs P. Kreuter. *Elephants & Ivory: Lessons from the Trade Ban* (London: Institute for Economic Affairs, 1994).

Taylor, Jerry. "The Challenge of Sustainable Development," *Regulation*, vol. 17, no. 1 (1994), pp. 35-50.

Wildavsky, Aaron. "Accounting for the Environment," *Accounting, Organizations and Society*, vol. 19, no. 4-5 (1994), pp. 461-481.

----------. *Searching for Safety* (New Brunswick, New Jersey: Transaction Books, 1988).

Yandle, Bruce, ed. *Land Rights: The 1990's Property Rights Rebellion* (Lanham, Maryland: Rowman & Littlefield, 1995).

----------. *The Political Limits of Environmental Regulation: Tracking the Unicorn* (Westport, Connecticut: Quorum Books, 1989).

Yandle, Bruce, and Roger E. Meiners, eds. *Taking the Environment Seriously* (Lanham, Maryland: Rowman & Littlefield, 1993).

The Competitive Enterprise Institute

The Competitive Enterprise Institute (CEI) is a public policy organization committed to advancing the principles of free enterprise and limited government. Founded in 1984 by Fred L. Smith, Jr., CEI promotes classical liberal ideals through analysis, education, coalition-building, advocacy, and litigation. A non-profit, tax-exempt organization under Section 501(c)(3) of the Internal Revenue Code, CEI relies entirely on donations from corporations, foundations, and private individuals. All contributions are tax deductible to the extent the law will allow.

For more information, contact:

Competitive Enterprise Institute
1001 Connecticut Avenue, N.W.
Suite 1250
Washington, D.C. 20036
phone: (202) 331-1010
fax: (202) 331-0640
E-mail: info@cei.org
Web site: http://www.cei.org